JACOB'S PILLAR

by

E. RAYMOND CAPT M.A., A.I.A., F.S.A. Scot.

Archaeological Institute of America

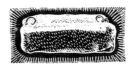

PUBLISHED BY

HOFFMAN PRINTING CO.
P.O. Box 1529
Muskogee, Oklahoma 74402
(918) 682-8341
www.artisanpublishers.com

PREFACE

The Scriptures are full of references to "stones", both literal and symbolic. One such stone, is identified as the stone upon which the patriarch Jacob rooted his head when he dreamed of the heavenly ladder. This stone has not received the attention it deserves from Bible scholars, because they generally assume it was left where Jacob found it.

However, this is not the case. The stone that Jacob later annointed with oil and declared to be "God's House" (Beth-El) did not remain lost in the wilderness of Luz; it continued to play an important part in the destiny of Jacob's descendants. In the past, such suggestions have been dismissed as fascinating legend and tradition, but there are pertinent historical writings and visible evidence worthy of consideration.

Is Jacob's stone the "House of God?" Does it exist today? Does it bear witness to God's amazing plan for our planet? The questions are puzzling. The answers are startling and throw light on the Bible. The purpose of this booklet is to present the cumulative evidence which reveals the fate of the Bible's most famous "stone".

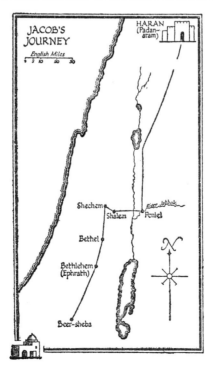

3

BETHEL.

THE STONE OF BETHEL

"*And Jacob went out from Beersheba, and went toward Haran.*

And he lighted upon a certain place, and tarried there all night, because the sun was set; and he took of the stones of that place, and put them for his pillows, and lay down in that place to sleep.

And he dreamed, and behold a ladder set up on the earth, and the top of it reached to heaven: and behold the angels of God ascending and descending on it.

And behold, the Lord stood above it, and said, I am the Lord God of Abraham thy father, and the God of Isaac: the land whereon thou liest, to thee will I give it, and to thy seed:

And thy seed shall be as the dust of the earth, and thou shalt spread abroad to the west, and to the east, and to the north, and to the south: and in thee and in thy seed shall all the families of the earth be blessed.

And behold, I am with thee, and will keep thee in all places whither thou goest, and will bring thee again into this land; for I will not leave thee, until I have done that which I have spoken to thee of.

And Jacob awaked out of his sleep, and he said, Surely the Lord is in this place; and I knew it not.

And he was afraid, and said, How dreadful is this place! this is none other but the house of God, and this is the gate of heaven.

And Jacob rose up early in the morning, and took the stone that he had put for his pillows, and set it up for a pillar, and poured oil upon the top of it.

And he called the name of that place Bethel: but the name of that city was called Luz at the first.

And Jacob vowed a vow, saying, If God will be with me, and will keep me in this way that I go and will give me bread to eat, and raiment to put on,

So that I come again to my father's house in peace; then shall the Lord be my God.

And this stone, which I have set for a pillar, shall be God's house: and of all that thou shalt give me I will surely give the tenth unto thee."
Gen. 28:10-22.

The Scripture deals chiefly with that which took place between Jacob and the Lord, as Jacob was making a journey from Beersheba to Padan-aram. Mention of a certain sunset and stones (plural) for pillows seem incidental, but suddenly one of those stones is brought into great distinction. The facts which brought that special stone into such prominence may be quickly read, for the Bible account of them is very short and their true symbolic importance is generally overlooked.

The veneration of sacred pillars was common in ancient Israel but no where in Scripture has an inanimate object been given such a glorious eminence, or divinely-declared purpose, as that which was bestowed on that "pillow-stone" upon which Jacob rested his head on that certain night. Jacob was so spiritually impressed that, to memorialize the occasion and the place, he blessed the stone on which his head had rested, sanctified it by anointing it with oil and. gave it the name "Bethel" (God's House). Although Jacob gave the name "Bethel" to the place, or locality, where the Stone was set up, he emphatically declared: *"The stone, which I have set for a pillar, shall be God's house."*

Twenty-two years passed, and Jacob was directed by the Lord to return to Bethel. In the interim, Jacob had been blessed not only with great riches but by a knowledge that at that place (Bethel) was his God. On his return, Jacob had a vision, and the Lord again spoke to him, saying, *"I am the God of Bethel"* (Gen. 31:13). Thus, the Lord associated Himself not only with the place of the vision but with the Bethel Stone, implying that He Himself inspired both the choice of this stone and its name.

After returning to Bethel, Jacob erected an altar of stones. And again God appeared unto Jacob and blessed him saying, *"Thy name is Jacob: thy name shall not be called any more Jacob, but Israel* (meaning "sons ruling with God"). *And God said unto him, I am God Almighty, be fruitful and multiply; a nation and a company of nations shall be of thee, and kings shall come out of thy loins* (Gen. 35:11, 12).

While the Bible account does not state explicitly that Jacob took the Bethel Stone with him when he journeyed from Bethel, it is hard to imagine that he would have simply left a monument with such remarkable associations to lie in the fields and be lost. Rather, it is most likely that this special Stone would be kept and venerated down through the ages.

There is Biblical evidence to show that the Bethel Stone was the inheritance of Joseph, committed to the care of the House of

Joseph. Jacob blessed each of his twelve sons before he died, in Egypt. But, while he was making the prophecy concerning Joseph and his house (to whom he had just given the "birthright") he stopped in the midst of his prophetic utterances and used the following parenthetical expression: *"from thence is the shepherd, the stone of Israel"* (Gen. 49.24).

"Thence", in this instance, is an adverb used as a noun, and is equivalent in value to "that place", or the place to which it refers. The phrase, "from thence", means "out of there, out from thither", (or) "out of that place". The place from whence (present form of the old word thence) the Stone came (Bethel) was part of the inheritance which fell to the House of Joseph when the land of Canaan was divided among the children of Jacob. This suggests that not only Bethel (the city or place) but also Bethel, the pillar-rock was given to the birthright family.

Approximately 215 years later, at the time of the Exodus, Jacob's descendants (or a large part of them) left Egypt under the leadership of Moses with all their possessions and much spoil besides. Jacob's "annointed" Stone must have gone out of Egypt with them, thereafter, accompanying them through their long forty-year trek through the wilderness.

Route of the EXODUS

The history and movements of Israel's wanderings in the desert-wilderness is a fascinating story. The Lord continually provided food for the Israelites during these forty years and twice it is recorded the Lord supernaturally provided them with water. The first incident mentioned was when the Israelites were encamped at Rephidem, where there was no water for the people to drink. Without previously selecting one special rock, the Lord said unto Moses: *"Behold, I will stand before thee there upon the rock in Horeb, and thou shalt smite the rock, and there shall come water out of it, that the people may drink"* (Exodus 17:6). The phrase, "there in Horeb", points out the place where the rock was at the time. If the Lord, when He spoke of the rock, had used the demonstrative form, and said, "that rock", then we should know that He was designating which one, or a certain one not yet selected, but the fact that He said "the rock", indicated to us that He was speaking of a rock with which they were already familiar. It was undoubtedly the Bethel pillar rock, "the shepherd, the Stone of Israel", which had been committed to the keeping of the house of Joseph.

The second instance was when the people were without water at Kadish, a city in the border of Edom, the area belonging to the descendants of Esau. At that place, the people of Israel were very bitter against Moses and Aaron and said unto them: *"And why have ye brought up the congregation of the Lord into this wilderness, that we and our cattle should die there? And wherefore have ye made us to come up out of Egypt, to bring us into this evil place? It is no place of seed, or of figs, or of vine, or of pomegranates; neither is there any water to drink"* (Num. 20:4, 5). Again, the Lord appeared unto Moses, saying: *"Take the rod, and gather thou the assembly together, thou and Aaron thy brother, and speak ye unto the rock before their eyes; and it shall give forth his water, and thou shalt bring forth to them water out of the rock: so thou shalt give the congregation and their beasts drink"* (Num. 20:8).

In both instances where the Lord provided water from the rock, there is not the slightest indication that there was any selection, or indication of preference for any certain rock in the vicinity of Kadish, or that one was not already chosen, and in their midst. It is clear, also, that at the very first mention of water for the people from this "rock", all that was necessary (as a preparatory measure) was for the Lord to say to Moses, "speak to the rock." Also, when the people were commanded to "gather before the rock", they clearly understood which rock it was, so that in all the great company, no explanations were necessary. Therefore, it must have been among them before this event, and well known to them.

Artists have depicted Moses standing by a great cliff from which water was pouring, showing the people drinking from the stream. However, this conception of the artist does not picture the actual scene, as described in the Bible. The same name, "the rock" was used at Rephidim and at Kadesh, thus showing the same rock was smitten at each location, although they are geographically many miles apart. Certainly the Israelites did not transport a cliff with them, but they did carry the Stone.

Jacob's Stone, or rock, was a type of Jesus Christ, who would bring forth living waters, welling up into eternal life. For proof, let us go back to the place called "Bethel." There we find that Jacob, after setting up the rock for a pillar, also anointed it with oil, which in sacred symbols is typical of the Holy Spirit. According to sacred history, this Bethel Stone is the only single stone that has ever been anointed; making it pre-eminently " the Anointed One." When Christ, the great prototype, came, and was anointed with the Holy Spirit, He was pre-eminent among men, "the Anointed One."

Also, concerning this "rock", which accompanied Israel, the Lord could say to Moses, "Speak to the rock." But, on the other hand, Israel also could say, concerning that Divine presence which went with them, "Let us sing unto the rock of our salvation." It is also said of Israel that they *"...did drink the same spiritual drink, for they drank of that Spiritual Rock that followed them and that Rock was Christ"* (I Cor. 10:4).

Jacob also called the Stone, "The Shepherd of Israel." And there is also a Divine One unto whom Israel prayed, saying, *"Give ear, O Shepherd of Israel."* Later, when this same Shepherd was manifest in the flesh, He said, *"I am the Good Shepherd"*, and His apostles spoke of Him as "The Great Shepherd" and "The Chief Shepherd." Since, with God, names are always characteristic, we would expect this Stone of Israel to be with Israel in all their wanderings. Hence, this "Shepherd" - though it be only a stone - as any other shepherd would do, must go with His flock.

Further, that the Scriptures might be fulfilled, Israel's Divine Shepherd-rock was smitten, for it is written, *"Smite the Shepherd."* So, too, Israel's literal Shepherd-rock was smitten. The Lord knew that He must be smitten for the sins of the people, and, that the type and prototype might agree, He gave the

9

command, *"Smite the rock."*

In view of God's miraculous intervention at their deliverance from Egypt, it should not be difficult to believe that the Children of Israel were supplied with water from that literal Rock, which went with them. It was their Shepherd-rock. Otherwise, how could, Moses, in asking permission for the Israelites to pass through the land of Edom, give assurances to the king of Edom, *"...we will not pass through the fields, or through the vineyards, neither will we drink of the water of the wells; we will go by the king's highway; we will not turn to the right nor to the left, until we have passed thy borders"* (Num. 20:17). The land they must have traverse was several hundred miles in lenght and would have taken a considerable lenght of time. However, Israel could afford to make this proposition, for both their Shepherd-rocks were with them (the literal and the spiritual). They knew that He, who had hitherto furnished them with food and water, would continue to supply them until the end of the journey. Otherwise, Moses would never have made such a promise.

True, there was a conditional promise made, in which there was a promise to pay for any of the water of Edom which Israel might use. This was made chiefly on account of the cattle which they might not always be able to control when passing by the cool and tempting water pools. During the heat of the day, this might prove to be a difficult task for the drivers; hence, the proviso.

THE STONE OF ISRAEL

After forty years of wanderings in the wilderness, the children of Israel entered unto the land of Canaan to establish the United Kingdom of Israel which had been founded at Sinai. A special stone or pillar plays an important part in the building of the House of God, known as "Solomon's Temple". Masonic tradition speaks of a stone called "Jacob's Pillar" (Encyclopedia of Freemasonry, 1921 Vol. II pg. 37 - Waite) which was rejected by the builders. Not only was this stone "in the rough" but it contained a crack which, possibly, could have split the stone in two pieces at any moment. It is further prophetically intimated that early in the building of the Temple the attention of the architects had been incidentally invited to this very stone, for use in the Temple. After inspecting the stone, the builders forthwith condemned it as unfit for any such purpose (Compare Ps. 118:22 and Acts 4:11).

Thus, "neglected and despised by the builders", it had remained in the Tabernacle. By the close of the seven and a half years Temple construction the stone had become practically forgotten. It seems always to have been used in Tabernacle worship for some religious purposes, but now that grander provisions had been made at Jerusalem for the ritual ceremony, it was clearly in danger of being set aside. Man had rejected the relic but God had provided otherwise. Just at the moment when the Tabernacle was to be taken down and packed up for the march to the Temple, silence reigning throughout the multitude, this stone appears to have given unmistakable evidence of its own peculiar and inestimable worth.

How the stone so suddenly, "became" of specific import, as to strike all concerned with astonishment and admiration, we do not know. We can only conjecture. Perhaps the stone itself may have spoken, for stranger things are recorded as facts in the Scriptures (Num. 22:21-35). At Kadesh, Moses had been directed to "speak" to this very same stone (Num. 20:7-13) and sinned by smiting it as he had at Horeb. This latter time he acted both in wrath and perhaps in pride, saying, *Shall we bring forth"?* —what, in reality, God alone could cause to flow. So, if the stone could "hear", why not "speak" upon some particular occasion? Jesus, when rebuked to quiet His followers on His triumphant ride into Jerusalem told the Pharisees, *"I tell you that, if these should hold their peace, the stones would immediately cry out"* (Luke 19:40).

At any rate, to continue Masonic tradition, some remarkable

11

incident occurred then and there at the Tabernacle. Whatever it was, it took place just before the sacred regalia started in procession to their place in the finished Temple of Solomon. The sentence was reversed, the stone could not be left behind to oblivion. Its indisputable identity and undoubted worth was made manifest to all. History is strangely silent and only scantily suggestive of these events and we may only imagine the circumstances of this occurrence and supply the shouts of those who witnessed them: "Lo, this is the Pillow of Jacob - The Dream Miracle Stone! It is the Stone of Israel, and Joseph is its guardian. Let it be borne in honor to the Temple of God!"

In the coronation of the kings of Israel we find, again, a special stone or pillar playing an important role. When Joash was brought forth and proclaimed the heir of David's Throne and was anointed King, the account states: *"And when Athaliah heard the noise of the guard and of the people, she came to the people into the temple of the Lord. And when she looked, behold, the King stood by a pillar, as the manner was"* (II Kings 11: 13, 14) In the Revised Standard Version it is rendered, "standing by THE PILLAR, as was their custom," the article "the" denoted a particular pillar, by, or upon, which it was the custom of Israel to crown their kings.

The Dr. Adam Clark translation reads, "stood on a pillar", which he explains is "The place or throne on which they were accustomed to put their kings when they proclaimed them." There is, in the Second Chronicles 23:13, a recapitulation of the circumstances concerning Joash, which gives the following, *"And she looked, and behold, the king stood at the pillar,"* again indicating that it was a particular pillar belonging to those who were anointed King.

The Companion Bible, in this instance, gives an alternate rendering as "UPON THE PILLAR". It is reasonable to assume that Joash stood UPON the stone which Jacob had set up, as a pillar, when he made his covenant with God. Israel was familar with the history of the Bethel Stone and knew it was the "House of God" to Jacob and that it had become the "Guardian Stone" of Israel. Thus, the King could have chosen no more fitting place for making his covenant to restore the law and its administration to Israel. It was a sacred stone and it had witnessed all of the many solemn compacts between God and His people.

The stone which was refused by the builders of Solomon's Temple did become the "head of the corner" as the pillar or Coronation Stone on which the kings of the House of David were crowned. The first attitude of the builders toward this stone was prophetic of the attitude and rejection of Jesus Christ by the Chief Priests and a majority of the people of the Nation of the Jews. The nation, at that time, was composed of a remnant of the House of Judah plus other races.

What happened to this Coronation Stone when the captivity of Israel took place starting 745 B.C.? The Bible purposely makes little mention of the Stone as such and then only in a secondary way, perhaps to guard against the tendency to make an idol of it. Also, it seems God intended for the identity of the Stone and the people connected with it to be hidden from the world for a time. However, it is logical to assume that the custody of the Stone would remain in the hands of some part of the people of Israel.

Between 745 - 721 B.C. we know the northern Ten-Tribed Kingdom of Israel (known as the House of Israel), together with a larger portion of the southern Kingdom of Judah (known as the House of Judah) were taken into Assyrian captivity (II Kings 17:3-6). Archaeological tablets found in the excavations of the Assyrian Royal Library at Nineveh have indicated that a majority of the Israelites escaped. Some traveled around the southern end of the Black Sea into the Danube River Valley and the Carpathian Mountains; others went by way of the Dariel Pass through the Caucasus Mountains, into the Steppes of Southern Russia.

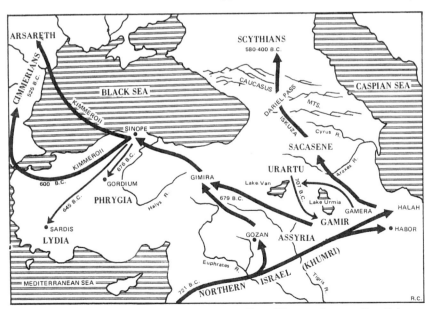

Israel – Gamera – Gimera – Kimmeroii – Cimmerians– Scythians

Confirmation of the escape of Israelites from Assyrian captivity is found in the writings of the Prophet Ezra (Esdras). After the ten tribes (House of Israel) refused the request of King Xerxes to return to Jerusalem to join the remnant of Judah from Babylon, Ezra (Esdras) wrote concerning their movements:

"And whereas thou sawest that he gathered another peaceable multitude unto him; Those are the ten tribes, which were carried away prisoners out of their own land in the time of Osea the king, whom Salmanasar the king of Assyria led away captive, and he carried them over the waters, and so came they unto another land. But they took this counsel among themselves, that they would leave the multitude of the heathen, and go forth into further country, where never mankind dwelt, That they might there keep their statutes, which they never kept in their own land. And they entered in to Euphrates by the narrow passages of the river. For the most High then shewed signs to them, and held still the flood, till they were passed over. For through that country there was a great way to go, namely, of a year and a half: and the same region is called Arsareth" (II Edras 13: 39-45).

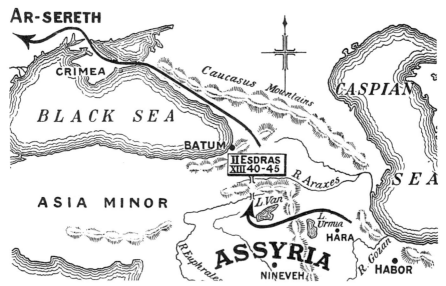

This is in harmony with the following: *"I will surely assemble, O Jacob, all of thee; I will surely gather the remnant of Israel; I will put them together as the sheep of Bozrah, as the flock in the midst of their fold: they shall make great noise by reason of the multitude of men. The breaker is come up before them: they have broken up, and have passed through the gate, and are gone out by it: and their king shall pass before them, and the Lord on the head*

of them" (Micah 2:12, 13).

The clause, *"They...have passed through the gate"*, and the one by Ezra, *"They have entered into the narrow passages"*, are parallel and refer to the same circumstance and place. This "gate", or "narrow passage", which is up among the headwaters of the Euphrates, is known today, as the "Caucasian Pass", or the "Pass of Dariel". Ancient writings sometimes refer to it as the "Pass of Israel". It is at this time that Hosea wrote: *"The children of Israel shall abide many days without a king, and without a sacrifice, and WITHOUT AN IMAGE"*, or as the marginal reading gives it, "WITHOUT A STANDING PILLAR". Young's Exhaustive Concordance, gives, among other definitions of the original Hebrew word, both "Memorial stone" and "pillar". Other authorities give us "pillar-rock" and "pillar-stone" as the correct rendering. All this justifies our conclusion, that the pillar in question is the Bethel Pillar Stone which was used as a Coronation Stone and retained by the royal family which ruled over the remnant of Judah until the overthrow of Zedekiah.

When Jerusalem was taken by the King Nebuchadnezzar of Babylon and the Temple destroyed, there was every probability that the Throne of David would become vacant. Zedekiah, the King of Judah had fled by night but was overtaken in the plains of Jericho where he and his sons were taken captive. Nebuchadnezzar killed all the King's sons. Then, after putting out the eyes of Zedekiah, took him in chains to Babylon where he later died in prison (Jer. 39:4-7). The king's DAUGHTERS were spared and there are several later references to them (Jer. 41:10-17 and Jer. 43:6).

Zedekiah's reign had lasted only about eleven years and he is considered by most Bible scholars to have been the last king of the Judo-David line to reign over any part of the Israel people. Yet God has said that He would build up David's Throne unto all generations. *"then I will establish the throne of thy kingdom upon Israel for ever, as I promised to David thy father, saying, There shall not fail thee a man upon the throne of Israel"* (I Kings 9:5), and prior to that He declared: *"The Sceptre shall not depart from Judah [his posterity] nor a law-giver from between his feet unto Shiloh come; and unto him [Shiloh] shall the gathering of the people be"* (Gen. 49:10).

Though that Throne ceased in Palestine when Zedekiah died, as a captive in Babylon, there must of necessity be a continuation of that throne. There must be a ruler of the House of David

15

reigning over at least a portion of the House of Israel, forever. Since Zedekiah's sons were killed there were no male heirs to the throne of Judah. However, under Hebrew law (Num. 27:8-11) a daughter would inherit as though she were a son and the right of descent would pass to her male seed, providing she married within her own house (Num. 36). This fact was evidently unknown to Nebuchadnezzar who thought that in slaying all the male heirs to the Throne of David it had been destroyed forever. The King's daughters, in the company of Jeremiah, did escape with a remnant of Judah to the land of Egypt. Jeremiah, with the daughters, found sanctuary with the Milesian (Greek mercenaries) garrison, which according to secular records, was stationed in Tahpanhes, Egypt (Jer. 43: 5-7).

Tahpanhes has been identified as the Greek fortress "Daphnae" (modern Tel Defneh), which is on the caravan road from Egypt to Palestine. For travelling and commercial purposes, the fortress was near the frontier of Egypt. However, after reaching the fort a traveler must traverse another 150 miles of waterless desert before reaching the gardens of Gaza.

Professor Sir W. M. Flinder Petrie (Professor of Egyptology at the University College, London, 1894) in the report of his excavations at Tahpanhes describes the fortress as having a central structure of brickwork 143 feet square and probably 30 to 40 feet high. From the top of this building a far watch over the desert plains could be maintained. The entire fortified camp was ringed with walls over 40 feet thick. The report also describes a royal apartment or palace opening into a wide paved area on the north-east of the fortress. Its purpose, Petrie concluded, was for Egyptian governors or other officials who might visit there. If so, then such accomodations would have been at the disposal of the royal Hebrew princesses. It is meaningful that Tell Defneh is also known to this day as "Qasr Bint el Yehudi", meaning "The Palace of the Jew's Daughter". So through the long ages of Greek and Roman and Arab there has come down the memory of the royal residence of the "King's daughters" from the destruction of Jerusalem.

We are now in a position to understand the politics of the time and the importance of Tahpanhes. It was build as a border fortress and manned by Greek mercenaries against the then rising power of the Assyrian Empire. It was therefore, the most natural thing for any Hebrews escaping from the vengeance of the Assyrians, to flee to the safety of the Greek garrison over the border. When Jeremiah and the Hebrew king's daughters were fleeing the

Babylonians they would have also fled to this nearby place of safety, and doubtless they would appeal to the King of Egypt for some help. Pharaoh-Hophra (otherwise called Apries by Herodotus; Uaphris by Manetho; Haa-ab-ra; Uehabre, and other variants of the name by modern authorities) had recently come to the throne in 589 B.C. One of his first acts had been to try to hold the south of Palestine in alliance with Judah. From there the Babylonians had beaten him off, when they destroyed Jerusalem in 588 B.C. So, to a fugitive royal party from Jerusalem, he might be expected to show friendship and good will.

The prophecies of Jeremiah are remarkable for their variety of application; Not only do these prophecies cover a lengthy period of time, extending from the then immediate future until the end of the age, but some of them also concern specific individuals. One such person was Pharaoh-Hophra whom Jeremiah foresaw would fall into the hands of his enemies and made his prophecy accordingly. Some time later Hophra was deposed and imprisoned by his subjects, but was well treated. After some years, he escaped and endeavoured to return to power, but on being opposed by the forces of the new Pharaoh, his own supporters murdered him, thus fulfilling Jeremiah's prophecy.

Hophra's successor, Aahmes, in driving the Greek settlers and garrisons out of Egypt for supporting his rival, thus weakened his country and prepared the way for Nebuchadnezzar's invasion predicted by Jeremiah: *"Behold, I will send and take Nebuchadnezzar the king of Babylon, my servant, and will set his throne upon these stones that I have hid...And when he cometh he shall smite the land of Egypt, and deliver such as are for death; and such as are for captivity; and such as are for the sword to the sword* (Jer. 43: 10,11).

Jeremiah also prophecied that the Israelites who fled to Egypt to escape the Babylonians would not escape God's judgment: *"Therefore hear ye the word of the Lord, all Judah that dwell in the land of Egypt: Behold, I have sworn by my great name, saith the Lord that my name shall no more be named in the mouth of any man of Judah in all the land of Egypt, saying, The Lord God liveth. Behold, I will watch over them for evil, and not for good: and all the men of Judah that are in the land of Egypt shall be consumed by the sword and by the famine, until there be an end of them"* (Jer. 44: 26,27). Following this judgment was the promise that a remnant would escape: *"For none shall return but such as shall escape"*(Jer. 44:14). indicating that a small remnant would escape the desolation and destruction soon to descend upon Egypt.

Earlier, God had promised Jeremiah: *"Verily it shall be well with thy remnant; verily I will cause the enemy to entreat thee well in the time of evil and in the time of affliction"* (Jer. 15:11). This statement is followed by the promise that Jeremiah would pass into a land which he did not know. *"And I will make thee to pass with thine enemies into a land which thou knowest not"* (Jer. 15:14).

Isaiah also tells us of the remnant that was to go forth from Jerusalem and escape: *"And the remnant that is escaped of the house of Judah shall again take root downward, and bear fruit upward"* (Isa. 37:31). This fits in with Jeremiah's Divine commission: *"See, I have this day set thee over the nations and over the kingdoms, to root out, and to pull down, and to destroy, and to throw down, to build, and to plant"* (Jer. 1:10).

This remnant which was to escape was not the remnant that was left by Nebuchadnezzar; nor the entire remnant that went down into Egypt to dwell, but Jeremiah's own particular little remnant, a small, select company that had been given to him to use in the "planting" and "building". Since this planting and building was to take place in a land that Jeremiah did not know, it could not have been in Egypt, Palestine, or Babylon, or any of the small nations around Palestine. The expression "to pass" is significant, for it implies travel by sea, passage by boat.

The Bible records Jeremiah fulfilling the first part of his commission but of the "building" and "planting" there is no record. That planting and building, moreover, was to be in a distant foreign land to which God declared Jeremiah would lead his remnant. Since the commission concerned the Throne of David, and as Jeremiah was instrumental in the removal of kings who did evil in the sight of God, it follows that the "building" phase of the prophecy would also be related to the Throne. Upon leaving Egypt, Jeremiah would doubtless have had in his possession the Stone of Bethel, the Symbolical Throne of David. The Stone was a witness of promises still to come, some of which even today are waiting fulfillment. Certainly, Divine Providence would not allow this witness to suffer destruction or fall into sacrilegious hands.

EZEKIEL'S RIDDLE

The Scriptures are silent concerning Jeremiah's whereabouts after describing his journey to Egypt. But, we have every reason to believe God would see to it that he was preserved to accomplish the building and planting which he was commissioned to do. The daughters of King Zedekiah became the prophet's wards. Because God had promised that His covenant with David would not be broken and that David would never lack a seed to reign upon his Throne, the building and planting obviously had to do with preserving this royal branch of the House of David.

This brings us to the all-important question; what happened to this Royal party after they left Egypt? Where did they go? One important clue is found in the riddle of Ezekiel, chapter 17: *"And the word of the Lord came unto me, saying, Son of Man, put forth a riddle, and speak a parable unto the house of Israel; And say, Thus saith the Lord God; A great eagle with great wings, long-winged, full of feathers, which had divers colours, came unto Lebanon, and took the highest branch of the cedar: He cropped off the top of his young twigs, and carried it into a land of traffick; he set it in a city of merchants. He took also the seed of the land, and planted it in a fruitful field; he placed it by a great waters, and set it as a willow tree. And it grew, and became a spreading vine of low stature, whose branches turned toward him, and the roots thereof were under him: so it became a vine, and brought forth branches, and shot forth springs"* (Ezek. 17:1-6).

These first verses of the parable introduce a "great eagle". It is used by the prophet to symbolize the Babylonian ruler, Nebuchadnezzar. He had succeeded to the sovereignty of the Gentile succession of empires (Dan. 2:31-45) destined to control the world during the absence of Israel from her own land. The eagle was an Assyrian emblem and this fact is probably referred to in Habakkuk 1:8. The eagle-headed deity of the Assyrian sculptures is that of the god "Nisroch". In the representations of battle scenes, trained birds of this order are frequently shown accompanying the Assyrian warriors into battle.

Nebuchadnezzar invaded Lebanon, home of the famous cedar trees, in southern Syria. This was the home of the Hebrew patriarchs after their migration from Mesopotamia, where Isaac and Jacob later obtained their wives. The Royal dynasty of Israel might be likened unto a great Cedar of Lebanon. The "highest branch" of the cedar and the "top of his young twigs" represent King Jehoiachin and the princes of Judah removed to Babylon in the "land of traffick". Nebuchadnezzar also took of the "seed of the land" and planted it "as a willow tree" in a fruitful field by greatwaters (Ezek.17:5). Vast numbers of willows line the waterways of Mesopotamia; the roots of the trees help to hold the mud banks together. In this respect, it is a fitting symbol of a country that depended for its existence upon irrigation and water-borne trade, as did Mesopotamia in general and Babylon in particular. After Jehoiachin was taken to Babylon, his brother Zedekiah was made a puppet ruler of Nebuchadnezzar.

Zedekiah was planted figuratively by the "great waters" of the Euphrates upon which he too was to depend for his existence. This "seed" of the cedar tree, planted like a "willow" of Babylon, "became a vine, and brought forth branches, and shot forth sprigs". Here is an ingenious intermingling of national symbols: the cedar, typifying the House of David, was set up to grow both as a Babylonian "willow" and as a "vine" which is the symbol of Joseph and the birthright. All this was done as part of Nebuchadnezzar's great plan to establish sovereignty over Israel. This puppet state became only a "vine of low statute". It could not compare with the former exalted state of the servant nation, for out of all 12 tribes of Israel only a badly shattered remnant of the Kingdom of Judah was left.

The riddle continues with the introduction of another great eagle: *"There was also another great eagle with great wings and many feathers: and behold, this vine did bend her roots toward him, and shot forth her branches toward him, that he might water it by the furrows of her plantation. It was planted in a good soil by great waters, that it might bring forth branches, and that it might bear fruit, that it might be a goodly vine. Say thou, Thus saith the Lord God; Shall it prosper? shall he not pull up the roots thereof, and cut off the fruit thereof, that it wither? it shall wither in all the leaves of her spring, even without great power or many people to pluck it up by the roots thereof. Yea, behold, being planted, shall it prosper? shall it not utterly wither, when the east wind toucheth it? it shall wither in the furrows where it grew.* (Ezek. 17:7-10).

The second "great eagle" was the Pharaoh of Egypt, who was approached by Zedekiah in hope of deliverance from the Babylonian king. The Egyptians sent a force to the assistance of the king of Judah, but it was defeated by Nebuchadnezzar's army. Zedekiah and all his sons were taken to Babylon to meet their unhappy end, and Jerusalem was destroyed. This was the dreadful fulfilment; the "roots" of the plant were torn up, and its fruit was "cut off". Zedekiah saw his sons slain in his sight, and then his own eyes were put out.

Ezekiel continues: *"Moreover, the word of the Lord came unto me saying, Say now to the rebellious house, Know ye not what these things mean? tell them, Behold, the king of Babylon is come to Jerusalem, and hath taken the king thereof, and the princes thereof, and led them with him to Babylon; And hath taken of the king's seed, and made a covenant with him: he hath also taken the mighty of the land: That the kingdom might be base, that it might not lift itself up, but that by keeping of his covenant it might stand. But he rebelled against him in sending him ambassadors into Egypt, that they might give him horses and much people. Shall he prosper? shall he escape that doeth such things? or shall he break the covenant, and be delivered? As I live, saith the Lord God, surely in the place where the king dwelleth that made him king, whose oath he despised, and whose covenant he brake, even with him in the midst of Babylon he shall die. Neither shall Pharaoh with his mighty army and great company make for him in the war, by casting up mounts, and building forts, to cut off many persons: Seeing he despised the oath by breaking the covenant, when, lo, he had given his hand, and hath done all these things, he shall not escape. Therefore thus saith the Lord God; As I live, surely mine oath that he had despised, and my covenant that he hath broken, even it will I recompense upon his own head. And I will spread my net upon him, and he shall be taken in my snare, and I will bring him to Babylon, and will plead with him there for his trespass that hath trespassed against me. And all his fugitives with all his bands shall fall by the sword, and they that remain shall be scattered toward all winds: and ye shall know that I the Lord have spoken it."* (Ezek. 17:12-21).

The second part of the parable (second great eagle) is set up in contrast to the first (first great eagle), which saw how the aspirations of the kings of Judah were brought to nought. Their failures, however, were not to be allowed to annul the promises of perpetuity made to the House of David. Despite the fact that the male succession to the throne apparently ended with the death of Zedekiah's sons, there was yet a method for the continuation of the royal line, the right of female succession as granted by Hebrew law. The allegory employed from verse 22 onwards of Ezekiel's riddle provides the feminine link: *"Thus saith the Lord God; I will also take of the highest branch of the high cedar, and will set it; I will crop off from the top of his young twigs a TENDER one, and will plant it upon an high mountain and eminent: In the mountain of the height of Israel will I plant it; and it shall bring forth boughs, and bear fruit, and be a goodly cedar: and under it shall dwell all fowl of every wing; in the shadow of the branches thereof shall they dwell. And all the trees of the field shall know that I the Lord have brought down the high tree, have exalted the low tree, have dried up the green tree, and have made the dry tree to flourish; I the Lord have spoken and have done it"* (Ezek. 17: 22-24).

In the grammatical structure of the text of verse 22, the words, "branch", "the high", "its" (the cedars) and "twigs" are feminine whereas the masculine could have been used in each case. These feminine words should be taken as being in some way prophetically connected. Since the "highest branch" refers to the royal family of Zedekiah; the "high cedar", the Royal House of David, it follows that the "tender twig" would indicate a female of the Royal family of Zedekiah. The King's daughters would have been the only individuals who were in a position to perpetuate the Davidic line.

With the end of the male succession on the Throne of David, as recorded in the Bible, we look for the continuation of that line in one of the "kings daughters" taken by Jeremiah into Egypt (Jer. 43:6). We are not told in the Scriptures how many king's daughters there were, or any of their names. Nor does the Bible give any historical narrative of what happened to these princesses beyond telling us that they were taken to Egypt with Jeremiah, Baruch (the scribe) and others. But, in our view, the prophetic parable that we are now considering may reasonably be taken as applying to one of them. Also, we may assume that the royal line of David would be re-established in Israel, in "an high mountain and eminent: in the mountain (future nation) of the height (Heb. 'high place') of Israel".

Now that the House of Judah was broken forever, the royal line was to be transferred to the House of Israel. This is entirely in keeping with the parables of the potter's vessels. The House of Judah was commanded by Jeremiah to get a potter's earthen bottle (fired pottery) with which he was to demonstrate the judgement upon Judah. Jeremiah was told to take some of the leaders among the people and the priests and go to the valley opposite the pottery - gate where he was to proclaim a message of judgement upon them for their evil ways. He was to then break the bottle in the sight of those who went with him and say to them: "Thus saith the Lord of hosts: Even so will I break this people and this city, as one breaketh a potter's vessel, that cannot be made whole again" (Jer. 19:11).

Contrasting the illustration of the House of Judah, the House of Israel's condition was that of a vessel of clay damaged in the making but still workable clay, capable of being reshaped. *"And the vessel that he made of clay was marred in the hand of the potter: so he made it again another vessel, as it seemed good to the potter to make it. Then the word of the Lord came to me, saying, O · house of Israel, cannot I do with you as this potter? saith the Lord, Behold, as the clay is in the potter's hand, so are ye in mine hand, O house of Israel"*(Jer. 18:4-6). (This illustration alone is sufficient to establish the House of Israel and the House of Judah as two separate and distinct peoples).

A further prophecy of the transferring of David's Throne from the House of Judah is found in Ezekiel 2: *"And thou, profane wicked prince of Israel, whose day is come, when iniquity shall have an end, Thus saith the Lord God; Remove the diadem, and take off the crown: this shall not be the same: exalt him that is low, and abase him that is high, I will overturn, overturn, overturn, it, and it shall be not more* (overturned), *until he* (the Messiah) *come whose right it is; and I will give it* (the Throne of David) *to him"* (Eze. 21: 25-27).

In the above prophecy of Ezekiel, the accepted interpretation of the "profane wicked prince", the one that was "high" is that he was Zedekiah, King of Judah. It is he who was to be brought down. But who was the "low" one referred to, who was to be exalted; the one that was ruled over at the time the words were spoken? To answer this question, it is necessary to return to an incident in the thirty-eighth chapter of Genesis, which is related with such explicit detail that it must be regarded as highly significant. Usually, in such cases, the dialogue foreshadows coming events.

In the Bible narrative, Judah, the son of Jacob, who was to be the father of the future kings of the covenant people, married a Canaanitish woman. But the Canaanites were an abomination to the Lord because of their Baal worship and other unrighteous practices. Therefore, none of the sons of this marriage were allowed to become progenitors of the promised royal line.

Two of the sons by this marriage died, and in the course of time the Canaanitish wife also died. Then, the Scriptures tell of how Tamar, a woman who had been living a celibate life for years, but who longed for motherhood, became the mother of twins of Judah. The recorded incidents concerning the birth of Judah's twin boys are also meaningful. The midwife in such case to distinguish the elder for the right of inheritance, had made ready a scarlet thread with which to mark the one who should be the rightful heir.

"And it came to pass, when she travailed, that the one put out his hand: and the midwife took and bound upon his hand a scarlet thread, saying, This came out first. And it came to pass, as he drew back his hand, that, behold, his brother came out: and she said, How hast thou broken forth? this breach be upon thee: therefore his name was called Pharez. And afterward came out his brother, that had the scarlet thread upon his hand: and his name called Zarah" (Gen. 38: 28-30).

There could be no other significance here than that both of these twins were to be inheritors of the birthright somewhere along the line of descendants. Naturally, Pharez, the first born, was to come first. It was from him that David, the first king from the tribe of Judah, descended (Saul, the first king over the Twelve Tribes was a Benjaminite). But the midwife said, *"This breach be upon thee".* Moffat translates this remark, *"What a breach you have made for yourself".* This would clearly indicate that somewhere in descent of the Pharez line there would be a break in the sequence.

The royal line of Pharez, established in David, was unbroken until the command of the Lord was given concerning Zedekiah, *"Take off the crown; exalt him that is low, and abase him that is high".* When Zedekiah was dethroned and all his sons were slain, there certainly was a breach in the line of Pharez, for not another king has reigned over the tribe of Judah. But, as we have seen, a daughter was to be planted in a distant land. However, the command was to exalt him that was "low", or the non-ruling line of Judah. This had to be Zarah, the Prince of the scarlet cord. In other words, the Zarah branch of the royal House of Judah, seemed destined to supercede the Pharez branch.

ZARAH, THE PRINCE OF THE SCARLET THREAD

There is very little in the Scriptures that applies specifically to Zarah, the Prince of Judah. His immediate posterity is given as follows: *"And the sons of Zarah; Zimri, and Ethan, and Herman, und Calcol, and Dara; five of them in all"* (I Chron. 2:6). Two of his descendants are given as authors of certain of the Psalms. And Solomon is described as having wisdom greater *"than Ethan, the Ezrahite, and Herman, and Calcol, and Darda* (I Kings 4:31). However, there is a bountiful supply of data in historical records, generally overlooked by Bible scholars, which sheds light on the fulfillment of Jeremiah's commission. It seems certain that the family of Zarah aspired to the sceptre of Judah but failed to attain their ambitions. After a time, Zarah's entire household seems to have migrated out of Palestine. Where the Scriptures allow the record of Zarah's line to lapse (we believe purposely), we find secular history provides the necessary clues. When properly fitted together, these enable us to blend the whole into one continuous recital down to the present day.

An examination of some of the historical clues reveals that Darda, "the Egyptian", (son of Zarah) was "Dardanus", the Egyptian founder of Troy: "Hecataeus, therefore, tells us that the Egyptians, formerly, being troubled by clamities, in order that the divine wrath might be averted, expelled all the aliens gathered together in Egypt. Of these, some, under their leaders Danus and Cadmus, migrated to Greece" (Fragmenta Historicorum, by Muller; vol. II, pg. 385 - copied from the works of Hecataeus of Abdera, a fourth-century B.C. Greek historian).

The "clamities" referred to were obviously the plagues which God brought down of the Egyptians, and the "aliens" were the Israelites, some of whom migrated to Greece with Danus and Cadmus, while others, under the leadership of Moses, made their exodus to the Wilderness of Sinai.

Diodorus gives us another version of the same story: "Now the Egyptians say that also after these events a great number of colonies were spread from Egypt all over the inhabited world...They say also that those who set forth with Danaus, likewise from Egypt, settled what is practically the oldest city of Greece, Argos, and that the nations of the Colchi in Pontus and that of the Jews (remnant of Judah), which lies between Arabia and Syria, were founded as colonies by certain emigrants from their country; and this is the reason why it is a long-established institution among these peoples to circumcise their male children, the custom having been brought over from Egypt. Even the Athenians, they say, are colonists from Sais in Egypt" (Diodorus of Sicily, by G.H. Oldfather, 1933, vol 1, bks 1—II, 1-34 pg. 91).

The descendants of Darda ruled ancient Troy for some hundreds of years, until the city was destroyed in the famous "Siege of Troy". Aeneas, the last of the royal blood, (Zarah-Judah), collected the remnants of his nation and traveled with them to Italy. There he married the daughter of Latinus, king of the Latins and subsequently founded the great Roman Empire. Aeneas' son (or grandson) Brutus, with a large party of the Trojans, migrated to Malta, and there was advised to re-establish his people in "the Great White Island" (an early name for Britain due to its chalk cliffs). This advice is recorded in an archaic Greek form on the Temple of Diana in Caer Troia (New Troy). An historic stone still stands in the town of Totnes, on the shores at Torbay, commemorating his coming (Circa 1103 B.C.). Brutus then made contact with his kindred blood in Britain and built for himself a new capital city to which he gave the name "Caer Troia", or New Troy. The Romans later called it "Londinium", now known as London.

The actual date of the founding of London is suggested in the Welsh bardic literature: "And when Brutus had finished the building of the city, and had strengthened it with walls and castles, he consecrated them and made inflexible laws for the governance of such as should dwell there peacefully, and he put protection on the city and granted privilege to it. At this time, Beli the Priest ruled in Judea, and the Ark of the Covenant was in captivity to the Philistines" (The Welsh Bruts).

The reference in the above quotation to Beli the Priest, is obviously of Eli of the first book of Samuel. Such remote prehistorical antiquity of the site of London is confirmed by the numerous archaeological remains found there, not only of the New Stone and Early Bronze Ages, but even of the Old Stone Age, thus indicating that it was already of settlement at the time when Brutus selected it for the site of his new capital of "New Troy".

According to "The Harmsworth Encylopaedia", Cecrops ("Calcol" of I Chron. 2:6 and "Chalcol" of I Kings 4:31, and brother of Darda) was the mythical founder of Athens and its first king. He was thought to have been originally a leader of a band of colonists from Egypt. Dr. R.G. Latham, the ethnologist, asserts:"Neither do I think that the eponymus of the Argive Danai was other than that of the Israelite tribe of Dan; only we are so used to confine ourselves to the soil of Palestine in our consideration of the history of the Israelites, that we treat them as they were 'adscripti glebae' and ignored the share they may have taken in the ordinary history of the world" (Ethnology in Europe, 1852, pg. 37).

Historical records tell of the westward migration of the descendants of "Calcol" along the shores of the Mediterranean Sea. establishing Iberian (Hebrew) trading settlements. One settlement now called "Saragossa", in the Ebro Valley in Spain, was originally known as "Zarah-gassa", meaning "The Stronghold of Zarah". From Spain they continued westward as far as Ireland. The Iberians gave their name to Ireland, calling the island "Iberne" which was later abbreviated to "Erne", and subsequently Latinised to "Hibernia", a name that stills adheres to Ireland.

Note that in pre-Exodus days Abraham's descendants were still called by their more ancient name "Hebrews: (See Exodus 2, 6, 13, etc.) or "Heberites" (Num. 25:45), being descended from "Heber" (spelled "Eber" in N.T. Scripture). Heber was Noah's great-great-grandson, and the great-great-great-great-grand-father of Abram or Abraham. Thus, the "Hibernians" or "Iberians" who came to Ireland about 1700 B.C. were undoubtedly Hebrews, descended from Abraham through Judah's son Zarah and grandson Calcol. Later history records that these people grew considerably and expanded into Scotland.

Many historical records point to Israel's presence (particularly Dan and Judah) in Ireland at a very early date. On Ptolemy's ancient map of Ireland we find in the north-eastern corner of the Island such names as "Dan-Sowar" (Dan's Resting Place) and "Dan-Sobairse" (Dan's habitation). Gladstone's "Juventus Mundi" and the "old Psalter of Cashel" both state that some of the Grecian Danai left Greece and invaded Ireland. Writers such as Petanius and Hecatoeus of Abdera (sixth century) speak of Danai as being Hebrew people, originally from Egypt, who colonized Ireland.

The "History of Ireland" (Moore) states that the ancient Irish, called the "Danai" or "Danes", separated from Israel around the time of the Exodus from Egypt, crossed to Greece and then invaded Ireland. The "Tuatha De Danann", means the "Tribe of Dan". The "Leabha Gabhala", or "Book of Conquests of Ireland" give their earlier name as "Tuatha De", meaning "People of God". The great Irish historiographer, Eugene O'Curry, says: "The De Danann were a people remarkable for their knowledge of the domestic, if not the higher, arts of civilized life". The ships of the Tuatha De Danann are accredited with bringing Jeremiah and Jacob's Pillar to Ireland.

Among the early records and chronicles of Ireland, those known as the "Planatation of Ulster" are the best preserved and most complete. They date back to about 700 B.C. and record the first important settlements of Hebrews in Ireland. One section of these chronicles are known as the "Milesian Records". They are named "Milesian" (meaning warrior) because they give an account of the genealogy and history of Gallam (William, the conqueror of Ireland), the last person mentioned in the genealogy. Among the names in the genealogy of Gallam are several that are specifically mentioned as belonging to the "Red" or "Scarlet" branch of Judah.

The Milesians invaded Ireland at about 1000 B.C. subjugating the De Danann. Most conquerors come to despise the conquered, but the Milesians came to honor, almost worship those whom they had subdued. Later generations of Milesians to whom were handed down the wonderful traditions of the De Danann they had conquered, lifted them into a mystic realm, the greatest ones becoming gods and goddesses, giving rise to the early belief that the people in question were mythological.

Both the De Danann and the Milesians were kinsmen, who long ages before, had separated from the main Hebrew stem. Many historians, today, erroneously refer to these people as "Celts" and "Gaels" whereas in fact, they were only forerunners of the Celtic tribes that wound their several ways across Europe from the East, turbulently meeting and finally blending in amity, and flowing onward in one great Gaelic stream into the Islands of Britain. The Celts were also kinsmen but mainly of the later westward migrations of the Israel tribes following their captivity in Assyria between 745 and 721 B.C..

It was Zarah's hand bound with a "scarlet thread" that probably accounts for the origin of the heraldic sign employed today in Ulster, northern Ireland, consisting of a Red Hand couped at the wrist with a scarlet thread. An ancient Irish record entitled "Cursory Proofs", lists five equestrian orders of Ancient Ireland. Among these five, one was called "Craobh-Ruadh (the Red Branch). The origin of this order was so ancient that all attempts at explanation have hitherto failed. These knights of the Red Branch called themselves "Craunogs", or the "Crowned". Undoubtedly these names have reference to the hand of the Prince of Scarlet Thread (Zarah).

THE FIRST "OVERTURN"

The story of Jacob's Pillar" may be likened to an arch, the left-hand span of which, starting at Bethel, carries us through Biblical history up to the destruction of Jerusalem about 584 B.C. The right-hand span of the arch begins at Westminster Abbey in Britain and reaches backwards to Tara in Ireland, just after 584 B.C. The Keystone upon which the story rests is the "first overturning" contained in Ezekiel's prophecy (Chapter 21:27). That takes the Stone from Jerusalem, after the city's destruction, to Tara.

From Bethel to Westminster is a long distance in both time and space. Any attempt to connect the two involves the necessity of reconstructing a consecutive, feasible story. There is a tradition that has subsisted from time immemorial, and is quoted in official guides, that the Stone of Scone, set in the Coronation Throne in Westminster Abbey, is none other than that on which the head of Jacob rested when he dreamed of the ladder with angels ascending and descending upon it. Is it just an interesting fable? Traditions do not spring from nothing, and this one is at least worthy of impartial examination.

The arrival in Ireland of the Bethel Stone rests upon the authority of the ancient records of Ireland and the traditions which abound there. Here let us understand that the ancient historical legends of Ireland are, generally speaking, far from being baseless myths. The Irish people are a people who eminently cling to tradition. Not only were the great happenings that marked great epochs enshrined in their memory, forever, but even little events that trivially affected the history of their race, were, and are, seldom forgotten.

The Irish poets and "seanachie (shanachy, the historian) of the remotest antiquity were honored next to the king, because of the tremendous value which the people set upon the recording and preserving of their history. The poet and the historian, following the fashion of the time, took advantage of their artist privilege to color their narrative to an extent that to the modern mind would seem fantastic. But it was with the details of the story that they were granted this liberty. The big, essential facts, had to remain unaltered. The things of importance no poet of repute, however highly he might color, could, or would dare to falsify. However strange are the story-tellers description of ancient tradition, when examined carefully provide substantial links which give credence to the basic truth of the traditions.

The modern part of the story from Westminster back to Ireland, rests on a succession of well authenticated Irish, Scottish and English historical documents which may be regarded as practically undisputed. Writers on the subject, quoting from such works as "The Chronicles of Eri", "The Annals of the Four Masters", "The Annals of Clonmacnoise", etc., locate the Stone originally at Tara, County of Meath, Ireland. Naturally, such early records as these are uncertain as to dates, but from the "MS Cambrensis Eversus" (by Dr. Lynch), published in Latin in 1662 and translated in 1848, the year circa 584 B.C. may be taken as the Tara starting date.

Scota was one of the earliest names of Ireland - so named, it was said, from Scota, the "daughter of the Pharaoh" one of the ancient female ancestors of the Milesians. These people were commonly called "Scotti" or "Scots", both terms being frequently used by early Latin historians and poets. The Irish legends also relate how this same "Scota" while in Egypt married "Gallo" (Gathelus), a "Miletus" (Milesian) chieftain, and that from this union the kings of Tara were descended. The marriage is said to have occurred during the reign of a Pharaoh who was "drowned" in the Red Sea. This would have been the Pharaoh-Hophra (XXVI Dynasty) who provided refuge to Jeremiah and the daughters of Zedekiah, and who was later murdered in his boat in 566 B.C.

The "Chronicles of Scotland" by Hector Boece (translated into Scottish by John Bellenden,1531), tell us the ancestor of the Scots was "ane Greyk callit Gathelus (father of Eochaidh, the Heremon, or Eremon), son (sometimes used to denote a descendant) of Cecrops (Calcol) of Athens, untherwayis of Argus, King of Argives", who came to Egypt when "in this tyme rang (reigned) in Egypt Pharo ye scurge of ye pepill of Israel". Gathelus gained a great victory for Pharo against "the Moris and Pepil of Yned" and "King Pharo gaif him his dochter, callit Scota, in marriage" (vol. I, pgs. 21-27). Neither the name or surname of Pharaoh is given but the word Pharaoh is the Egyptian term for "king" or "monarch". The fact that the records called Scota the Pharaoh's "daughter" is proof that they knew her as merely "the King's Daughter".

The Chronicles of Scotland continue the story of Gathelus, recording that he left Egypt with his wife (Scota), his friends and a company of Greeks and Egyptians rather that "to abyde ye manifest wengenance of goddis" (reference to God's judgment on the remnant that had fled to Egypt to escape Nebuchadnezzar) and, travelling by sea (Mediterranean), after, "lang tyme he landit in ane part of Spayne callit Lusitan" (later called Portingall). After this, he built the city of Brigance and "callit his subdittis (subjects) Scottis in honour and affeccioun of his wyiff". And, peace having been secured, "Gathelus sittand in his chayr of merbel within his citie".

This chair of "marble" had such fortune and omen that wherever it was found in any land the same land "shall become the native land of the Scots":

> The Scottis sall ioyis and brouke the landis haill
> Quhair yai fynd it, bot gif weirdis faill."

Translation:

> "The Scots shall brook that realm as native ground
> if words fail not, where'er this chair is found."

It should be noted that "The Students English Dictionary" defines "marble" as "any species of calcareous stone susceptible of a good polish". It is reasonable to assume the "marble chair" referred to was the Coronation Stone or the Bethel Stone, still in the hands of the sons (descendants) of Jacob when in the care of Gathelus and his Queen Scota.

Many of the ancient Irish records, when making reference to an "eastern king's daughter", also mention an old man; "a patriarch, a saint, a prophet", called "Ollam Fodhla" and his scribe-companion called "Simon Brug, Brach, Breack, Barech, Berach", as it is variously spelled. Reportedly, they carried with them many ancient relics. Among these were a harp, an ark or chest, and a stone called, in Gaelic, "Lia-Fail (pronounced Leeah-Fail), meaning "Stone of Fate" or "Hoary of Destiny".

Tradition asserts that Ollam Fodhla was none other than Jeremiah, the prophet; that the king's daughter was the heir of Zedekiah, the last king of Judah. Simon Brug (Baruch) was Jeremiah's scribe who figures prominently in Biblical history, and the harp was the one belonging to King David. The ark or chest was the Ark of the Convenant. Finally, that the stone, "Lia Fail" was the stone that Jacob anointed with oil at Bethel.

One story relating to Scota tells of her son, named "Eochaidh" (later called Eremhon or Heremon, meaning King) marrying a girl named "Tea Tephi." The following account, found in the "Annals of the Kingdom of Ireland by the Four Masters," states: "Tea (sometimes spelled Teah), the daughter of Laghaldh, son of Ith, whom Eremhon married in Spain was the Tea who requested of Eremhon a choice hill as her dower, in whatever place she should select it, that she might be interred therein. The hill she selected was Druimcaein, i.e., Teamhair (in Ireland)" (Vol. 1 pg. 31).

In the "Chronicles of Eri", by Milner, we find Eochaidh, the husband of Tea Tephi, associated with the Stone Lia Fail. The account is titled, "The Story of Lia Fail", and states: "In the early days it was carried about by priests on the march in the wilderness (hence the much-worn rings still attached to it, one at each end). Later it was borne by the sea from East to West-'to the extremity of the world of the sun's going' (an expression used by the Romans to describe Britain). Its bearers had resolved, at starting, to 'move on the face of the waters, in search of their brethren.' Shipwrecked on the coast of Ireland, they yet came safe with Lia Fail...Eochaidh 'sent a car for Lia Fail, and he himself was placed thereon."

The story of the Stone was then repeated by his order, "And Erimionn (Heremon) was seated on Lia Fail, and the crown was placed upon his head, and the mantle upon his shoulders, and all clapped and shouted." And the name of that place, from that day forward, was called "Tara" (spelled "Tamhra" in the Irish language). The fact that the story of the Stone was repeated by his (Eochaidh) order suggests definitely that this Stone was of ancient origin and custom, quite possibly of the earliest Israelites.

Another version lists Tea Tephi as being the daughter and heir of King Zedekiah (Scota, her younger sister, having married in Spain) who accompanied Jeremiah to Ireland to meet and marry Eochaidh. In this version Tea was made Queen at her husband's coronation (by Jeremiah) on the Stone of Bethel. The name of the capital is said to have been changed from "Lothair" to "Tara" and the Harp of David became the national emblem.

There are many other variations of the story of the Stone being brought from Egypt to Ireland, which when added together present us with a rather confused story. This is understandable when it is realized that the Irish records are compilations at a late date of very early tribal histories. Each of these, written in a tongue difficult to translate, gives its own aspect of the one great story. However, they all agree in the following: The Stone, known as the "Stone of Destiny", came from Spain, and before that, from Egypt, It came in the company of an aged guardian, who was called "Ollam Folla (Hebrew words that mean "revealer", or "prophet"). Eochaidh (Eremhon) with his Queen Tea Tephi was crowned King of Ireland upon the Stone which remained at the Palace of Team-hair Breagh. It was the Coronation Stone of every "Ard-Righ" (High King) of "Eireann" for a period of about 1040 years; from King Eremhon (The Heremon) to the 131st Ard-Righ, named "Murcheartach."

Tara, attained the climax of its fame umder Cormac, (the son of "Art, the lonely" and grandson of "Conn, of the Hundred Battles") who reigned as High-King in the third century. Cormac is unquestionably considered greatest by the poets, the seanachies, and the chroniclers. The noted 17th century Irish historian, O'Flaherty says: "Cormac exceeded all his predecessors in magnificence, munificence, wisdom, and learning, as also in military achievements. His palace was most superbly adorned and richly furnished, and his numerous family proclaim his majesty and munificence; the books he published, and the schools he endowed at Temair (Tara) bear unquestionable testimony of his learning. There were three schools instituted, in the first the most eminent professors of the art of war were engaged, in the second, history was taught, and in the third, jurisprudence was professed."

In Cormac's day, Tara must have been impressive. The great, beautiful hill was dotted with seven duns, and in every dun were many buildings - all of them of wood or of wood and metal. The greatest structure there was the "Mi-Cuarta", the great banqueting hall, which was in the Ard-Righs's own dun. It was probably the largest building of its time in either Great Britain or Ireland, measuring 700 feet in length and about 90 feet across. There the chiefs and their ladies listened to the stirring strains of the "harp that once through Tara's halls did play."

There was also the "House of a Thousand Soldiers", the ancient poets tell us. Each of the provincial kings had, on Tara, a house that was set aside for him when he came up to attend the great Parliament. There was a "Grianan" (sun house) for the provincial queens, and their attendants. The "Stronghold of the Hostages" was one of the structures. Another was the "Star of the Bards" - a meeting-house for the poets and the historians, the doctors and judges.

"Great, noble and beautiful truly was our Tara of the Kings" was the theme of the hundreds of ancient poets who sang the praises of Tara. Those words were not someone's fanciful imagination. Proof of this is found in the silent testimony of recently unearthed kingly ornaments. In recent times the archaeologists have turned up, among others, two splendid gold torcs (bands of twisted gold worn around the neck); one of them was five feet seven inches in length, weighing twenty seven ounces. The other band was of large size also, and weighs twelve ounces. Both of them are beautifully wrought.

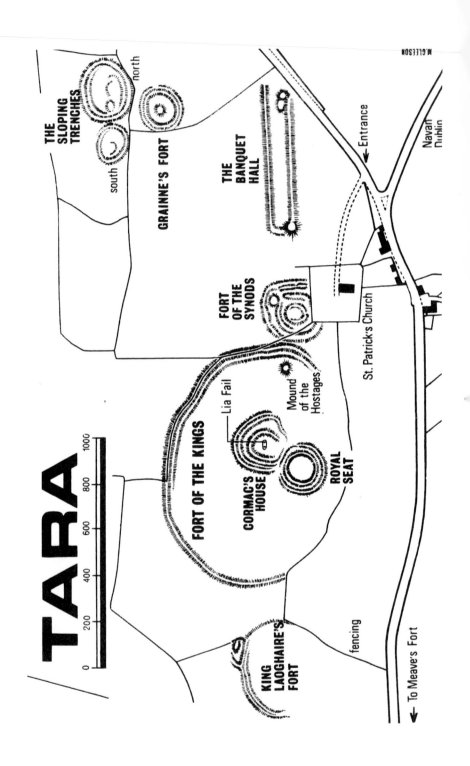

TARA

THE SLOPING TRENCHES

GRAINNE'S FORT

north

south

THE BANQUET HALL

FORT OF THE SYNODS

FORT OF THE KINGS

Lia Fail

CORMAC'S HOUSE

Mound of the Hostages

ROYAL SEAT

KING LAOGHAIRE'S FORT

fencing

To Meave's Fort

St. Patrick's Church

Entrance

Navan
Dublin

M.GLEESON

0 200 400 600 800 1000

34

Archaeological excavations on the mounds at Tara have also revealed that ancient Tara was not only the Royal Seat or Capital of the Celtic Kings, that came from Spain, but it was also the nerve center of the country. Five great arteries or roads radiated from Tara to the various parts of the country - The "Slighe Cualann", which ran toward the present County Wicklow; the "Slighe Mor", the great Western road, which ran via Dublin to Galway; the "Slighe Asail", which ran near the present Mullingar; the "Slighe Dals", which ran Southwest; and the "Slighe Midluachra", the Northern road. In order to cross the great central bogs, tracks were sometimes constructed of timber, laid on the peat, known as "tochan." This term is still extant in place-names such as "toghee."

AERIAL VIEW OF THE HILL OF TARA

It is worthy of note that the name "Tara" is the English corruption of the Irish word commonly written "Teamhara", which is the genitive of "Teamhar" or "Tamar." The final "a" has been aspirated according to the Hebrew rule of pronounciation, which in Irish has been extended to apply to the letter "m." In this form it almost disappears, making a sound like "Tea-wra, which to English ears becomes "Tara." Since Tara, is the genitive of "Tamar", it never stands alone, because being a genitive, it must be by another noun. Thus the great palace of Ulster, designed by

35

Queen Tea (Tamar), displaying a form of architecture which made it for centuries the wonder of Ireland, was called simply, "Tigh Teamhara", the "House of Tamar."

The name Tamar itself is also spelled "Thamar" in Matt. 1:3. Where there is translation of words from Hebrew into Greek the letter "h" is often dropped or added, i.e., we find "Eber" (Gen. 10:21) called "Heber" in Luke 3:35. Likewise we find Abraham's father "Terah", called "Thara" in Luke 3:34, which could with equal authority have been translated "Tara."

The name Tamar is found in many places in Britain. For instance the river dividing the two counties Devon and Cornwall is called the River Tamar. Tamar, according to "Cornish Directories" is derived from the same root as that of the river Thames. The latter is called "Tamise" in French, pronounced without sounding the letter "h", as in English.

Many bards have sung of Tara's halls, but one "Amergin", chief bard to King Dermod, a sixth century monarch or Ireland, wrote of Tea Tephi:

> "A rampart raised around her house,
> For Teah, the daughter of Lughaidh,
> She was buried outside in her mound,
> And from her it was named Tea-Mur."

"Lug" (or Log), is Celtic for "God", and "Aidh" is the same for "House", hence Tea Tephi is called "the daughter of God's House." Since Tea accompanied the Stone of Bethel (God's Stone), to the people of Ireland, she could have been none other than "the daughter" of that "House."

A celebrated bard, "Cu-an O'Cochlain", for a time Regent of Ireland (A.D. 1024), collected the legends which in his day were prevalent concerning Tara, and ran them into a poetic selection, from which is taken the following:

> "The gentle Heremon here maintained
> His lady, safe in an impregnable fortress;
> She received from him all the favors she desired,
> And all his promises to her he fulfilled.
>
> Bregli of Tea was a delightful abode,
> On record as a place of great renown;
> It contained the grand, the great Mergech,
> A sepulcher which has not been violated.

36

The daughter of Pharaoh, of many champions,
Tephi, the most beautiful that traversed the plains,
Here formed a fortress, circular and strong,
Which she described with her breast pin and wand.

She gave a name to her fair fortress,
This royal lady of agreeable aspect,
'The Fortress of Tephi', where met the assembly,
Where every proceeding was conducted with priority.

It may be related without reserve,
That a mound was raised over Tephi as here recorded,
And the bier beneath this unequaled tomb,
Here formed for this mighty queen.

**

It is a mystery not to be uttered.
The length and breadth of the tomb of Tephi,
Accurately measured by the sages,
Was sixty two feet of exact measure,
As prophets and Druids have related.

Tephi was her name! She excelled all virgins!
Wretched for him who had to entomb here;
Sixty feet of correct admeasurement,
Were marked as a sepulchre to enshrine her.

It is asserted that all mankind may know -
That a mound was raised over Tephi as recorded.
And she lies beneath this unequaled tomb,
Here formed for this mighty Queen.

**

A meeting was held to select a sepulchre,
In the South, as a tomb for the beloved Tephi;
Temor, the impregnable, of lasting resources,
Which conferred on the woman high renown."

   The above legend describes Tephi as the "daughter of
Pharaoh" whereas most of the ancient Irish Records and
Chronicles give her as the daughter-in-law of Scota, the daughter
of Pharaoh (as explained previously). Such a discrepancy is
understandable considering the time span in which the legend has
been handed down, and in no way discredits the basic story.

There is manifestly a mystery surrounding the burial of Tea Tephi. The great "Mergech", the name given the tomb of Tephi was once thought to be Celtic, but is now known to be Hebrew and significant. It designates a place of deposit for treasures, secrets, mysteries, etc. Considering the treasures: Ark of the Covenent, Title Deeds to Palestine and various other relics or Hebrew marks of identity that Jeremiah could have had in his custody, the explicitness with which this tomb of Tephi is described is noticable. Jeremiah 32: 13-44 records "evidences" which God directs Jeremiah and Baruch to bury.

(The actual burial site of Tea Tephi is unknown today. However, the author has seen a stone at Tara with significant markings which suggests that it marks the grave-vault of Ireland's first Queen of the Davidic line. Perhaps, in due time, the grave will be opened and the royal harp along with other relics will provide the evidence to convince all that God kept His Covevant with David. II Sam. 7:13).

Tradition has it that the Harp of David was brought to Ireland by Jeremiah and is buried with Tea Tephi at Tara. It is a significant fact that the royal arms of Ireland is a representation of the Harp of David, and has been such for 2500 years. This first mention of the Harp is found in the Dinn Leanches, by Mac Awalgain (B.C. 574).

Irish Free State   Eire

Vincenzio de Galilei (the elder) in his "Dialiga della Musica" (1581 A.D.) mentions that the harp of Ireland owes its origin to the Harp of David: "This most ancient instrument (commemorated Dante) was brought to us from Ireland where such are most excellently worked and in a great number; the inhabitants of the said island have made this their art during the many centuries they have lived there and, moreover, it is a special undertaking of the kingdom; and they paint and engrave it in their public and private buildings and on their hill; stating as their reason for so doing that they have descended from the royal Prophet David."

The Irish harp was, and is, a many-stringed instrument, and many harps of similar shape and stringing have been unearthed at Ur in Mesopotamia dating back to 2800 B.C. The "Clarsach" or "Highland Harp" of Scotland is a descendant of the early Irish harps as is the "Cruith" or "Clanseach" introduced into Wales (1098 A.D.) by Griffith, King of North Wales, who was born in Ireland. In 1565, Buchanan, writing of the Western Isles, says, "...they delight very much in music, especially in harps of their own sort, of which some are strung with brass wire, others with the intestines of animals. They ornament their harps with silver and precious stones; the lower ranks deck theirs with crystal."

GOLD AND MOSAIC HARP FROM UR OF THE CHALDEES

If harps were strung with wire, they were held on the left side plucked with nails grown long, the left hand taking the treble; if strung with gut, the harp was held against the right shoulder and struck with the cushion of the fingers, the right hand taking the treble. Strings were tuned by turning the pins with a key-in Gaelic, "crann". Should the player of a wire-stringed harp displease, his punishment was to have his nails cut.

The burial place of Ollam Fodhla (Jeremiah) is claimed as being in two different places. One is a tomb hewn out of rock in a cemetery on Devenish Island, in Lough Erne. It has been known from time immemorial as "Jeremiah's Tomb". The other, and best authenticated is located in Schiabhla - Cailliche, near Oldcastle,

County, Meath, in Ireland, not far from Tara. A huge cairn of stones marks the spot, and a large carved stone is still pointed out as Jeremiah's judicial seat. Some thirty stones with strange markings upon them, lie in the sepulchral chamber within the cairn. The markings consist of a jumble of lines, circles, dots and spirals.

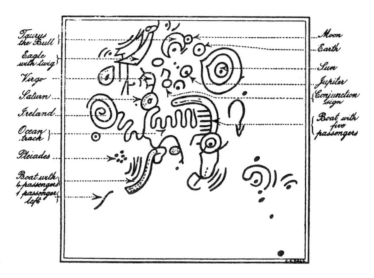

One interpretation of the hieroglyphics (by George Dansie of Bristol) is that they show a Lunar Eclipse, in the constellation of Taurus and a conjunction of the planets Saturn and Jupiter in Virgo. The prow of a ship is shown in the center, with five lines indicating the number of passengers it carries. On the left, a part of the ship, perhaps the stern, is shown with only four passengers, one having been left behind or lost as indicated by the line falling away from the ship. The wavy line indicates the passage of the ship across the ocean, terminating at a central point on an island.

A stellar calculation was made (by V.E.Robson, a friend of Dansie) of the astronomical interpretation of the hieroglyphics. This calculation established the date of Thursday, October 16, 583 B.C., a date consistent with the stellar calculations of the mysterious inscriptions.

Assuming Ollam Fodhla having been identified as Jeremiah, the inscriptions could have been a record of his journey from Egypt to Spain, having in his care the two daughters of King Zedekiah. With them was Baruch, Jeremiah's secretary and probably an attendant for the two Princesses. That fifth passenger might have been "Ebed-melech," the Ethiopian, that figures in some of the

40

traditions. Illustrating a second part of the boat indicated another voyage of Jeremiah and a party of four, to Ireland.

Some authorities on Irish history have cited the "Annals of the Kingdom of Ireland by the Four Masters" (edited from MSS. in the Library of the Royal Academy and of Trinity College, Dublin-translated by John O'Donovan, M.T.I.A.) as a link between Ireland and Jeremiah: "Ollam Fola (Foldha) is celebrated in ancient history as a sage and legislator, eminent for learning, wisdom and excellent institutions, and his historic fame has been recognized by placing his medallion in 'basso relievo' with those of Moses and other great legislators in the interior of the dome of the Four Courts of Dublin...The ancient Records and Chronicles of the Kingdom were ordered to be written and carefully preserved at Tara by Ollam Fola and there formed the basis of the Ancient History of Ireland, called the Psalter of Tara" (pg. 297).

The Four Courts of Dublin, which was destroyed by fire some years ago, did have a large dome decorated with large medallions of the world's greatest lawgivers. They included Alfred, Solon, Confucius, Moses and Ollam Fodhla. However, the "Ollam Fodhla" included in the medallions may not have been Jeremiah. The word "Ollam" means a learned man, and "Fodhla" was often used to indicate a "king". On the medallion, Ollam Fodhla appears, wearing a crown, but Jeremiah was not crowned. More likely, the Ollam Fodhla of the medallion was Eochaidh, the son of Scota.

The name "Ollam Fodhla" is found linked to Eochaidh in a further account given in the "Annals of the Kingdom of Ireland by the Four Masters": "Ollamh Fodhla after having been forth years in the sovereigny of Ireland died at his own house at Teamhair...Eochaidl was the first name of Ollamh Fodhla, and he was called Ollamh because he had been first a learned Ollamh, and afterwards King (Fodhla of Ireland" (Vol I, pgs 53-55).

41

OLLAM FODHLA'S [JEREMIAH'S] CAIRN
Lough Crew Hill, near Oldcastle, co. Meath

The crowning of Eochaidh, the son of Scota (daughter of Zedekiah) on the Stone of Destiny completed the first "overturn". This fulfilled the prophecy of the "high tree" (House of Pharez) being brought down and the "low tree" (House of Zarah) being exalted. In addition it completed Jeremiah's mission "to build and to plant" a seed of David's line through Pharez which would again "take root" and "bear fruit". In other words, that which had been the subject of prophecy concerning Jeremiah's commission, and his royal charge, is now recorded as a matter of history.

There are some who may object offhand, without knowledge, that an assignment of a Jacob-Luz origin to the Coronation Stone of Ireland is a matter of mere modern theory, the outgrowth of speculation. But this is an untenable position, for it has been known as Jacob's Stone dating back to the earliest Irish traditions. In the "Encyclopedia Britannica (Eleventh Edition-Vol 14, pg 569, under "Inisfail", the following is stated: "Inisfail, a poetical name for Ireland . It is derived from "Faul" or "Lia-fail", the celebrated stone, identified in Irish legend with the stone on which the patriarch Jacob slept when he dreamed of the heavenly ladder. The Lia-fail was supposed to have been brought to Ireland by the Dedannans and set up at Tara as the "inauguration stone of the Irish kings...Inisfail was thus the island of the Fail, the island whose monarchs were crowned at Tara on the sacred inauguration stone".

THE SECOND "OVERTURN"

About A.D. 500 some imigrants led by Fergus Mor McErc (the Great), from the Irish Gaelic Kingdom of Dalriada, invaded the Western coasts of Scotland, the land of the Picts. In George Buchanan's "History of Scotland", we read where Fergus of Ireland, after invading Scotland and returning home (Ireland) victorious: "the Scots confirmed the Kingdom (Scottish Dalriada) to him and his posterity by an oath" (Vol. I pg. 160). Being a believer in the old prophecy attached to the Stone of Destiny called Lia Fail, that, "wherever the Stone is found the Scottish race will reign" Fergus desired that he be crowned upon the Stone.

Dr. Geoffrey Keating records the circumstances surrounding the Stone Lia Fail being transported to Scotland: "When the race of Scots heard that the stone had this virtue (to roar), after Fergus the great, son of Earc, had obtained power of Scotland, and after he proposed to style himself King of Scotland, he sends information into the presence of his brother Muircheartach, son of Earc, of the race of Eiremhon, who was the King of Ireland at that time, to ask him to send him this stone, to sit upon, for the purposes of being proclaimed King of Scotland. Muircheartach sends the stone to him, and he is inaugurated King of Scotland on the same stone, and he was the first King of Scotland of the Scottish nation" (Forus Feasa ar Erim-Vol 1 pg. 207).

Andrew of Wyntown (1400 A.D.) in his ancient "Chronykil of Scotland", gives the following account of the stone of Destiny:

"Agret stane this kying then had
That fore this kynyes gete war made,
And haldyne wer a gret Jowal
Wyhthin the kynrky of Spayne hale
This kyng bad this Simon ta
That stane and in-tye ga,
A wyn that land and occupy
And halde that stane perpetually.
Fergus Erc, son fra hym syne
Down discented evyn be lyne
In to the five and fifty gre,
As every ne rechn and man may see
Broucht this stane wytht-in Scotland,
Fyrst guhen he come and wane that land.
* * *
Now will I the werd rehere

43

As I fynd of that stane in vers:
"In fallat fatum Scoti quotumque in locatum
In venient lapidem, regnare tenentur ibidem"

(Wyntown Chronykyl lib. III cap. 16)

The above account may be put into more modern English as follows:

"This king had at that time a famous stone which was used as his throne, and was regarded as a priceless jewel in Spain. He gave it to Simon, and directed him to take it with him to Ireland and win that country for occupation, and to hold the stone-throne perpetually. Fergus Earcus, a lively descendant of Simon in the fifty-fifth generation as on reckoning one may readily see (genealogy of Victosia Heremon to Fergus inclusive records 54 generations, add one for the father of Heremon, who is here represented as conferring it - 55 in all), brought the stone to Scotland, when he first came over and conquered it".

When the Stone of Destiny landed on Scottish soil, it constituted the second "overturn"; the first being its removal from Palestine, through Egypt and Spain to rest in Ireland. Undoubledly the Stone was set up a Dunadd, a hill-top fort, where Fergus established his capital. Although several miles inland today, in ancient times a navigable river ran by the hill to the sea. It was at Dunadd that Fergus was crowned King of Scotland on the Stone of Destiny. Near the top of Dunadd is a large flat rock. On the surface is a basin cut into the rock, a deeply carved footprint and a fainter barefoot mark, which may have been connected with coronation ritual. Tradition had that the newly crowned king would place his foot in the footprint as an indication that he would follow the precepts of his forefathers.

Also on the rock face are inscriptions, legible but cryptic. Several lines of Ogam script, consisting of short upright with diagonal lines above, begin near the snout of a carved Boar's head. Ogam script was invented in Ireland and used throughout Scotland about the 4th to 9th centuries A.D. Little remains now of the once defensive enclosures upon the summit of the hill. There is no trace remaining of the timber structures of the early inhabitants. The two wells that supplied their water still exist, one of which still produces water.

Dunadd, before becoming the capital of the Celtic Scots from Ireland, may have been a Pictish fort built to oppose the Celtic invaders from the sea as well as the hills. The remains of a net-work of ancient hill-top forts have been found of various designs and types. They seem to serve different purposes: to guard passes or landings; to watch for distant signals; or to provide refuge for a few families and to protect cattle from wolves. Archaeological excavations indicate Dunadd had been occupied from Middle Stone Age times.

The Picts (or in Gaelic, "Cruithne", meaning "Pictured Men", because they painted themselves) were a confederation of Celtic tribes, mainly in the north and east. They spoke a slightly different language than Celtic and having different customs from the Gaels of the west and the Britains of Strathclyde, though all were Celts (originally Cimmerians). Unlike the Scots who were pure nomads in those days, the Picts had fixed homes. They tilled the soil; raised crops; tended their cattle on their own pasture land. Often confused with the Picts are the Caledonians, another branch of the same people.

For a time Dalriada appears to have been dependent upon Irish Dalriada, but about 575 A.D. Aidan (son of Gabran, king of Dalriada) secured its independence and was crowned King of Scotland upon the "Stone Lia Fail." For this occasion, the Stone was taken to Iona (a tiny island of the Inner Hebrides), Scotland by St. Columba, the missionary grandson of Fergus the Great. Iona is where Columba founded his first Scottish monastery. It was famous as a center of Celtic Christianity from where missionaries were dispatched for the conversion of the pagan tribes in Scotland and Northern England.

Aidan was crowned King of Scotland in a coronation rite that has been used ever since by the succeeding monarchs of Scotland and England. The ritual included a consecration declaring the future of Aidan's children, grandchildren, and great - grandchildren, exactly as was done by Jacob when he blessed his sons before he died.

Columba seems to have had the gift of prophecy, for apart from declaring the future of Aidan's posterity, he seems to have foretold the future of Iona in these words: "Unto this place, small and mean though it be, great homage shall yet be paid, not only by the kings and peoples of the Scots, but by rulers of foreign and barbarous nations and their subjects. In great veneration too, shall it be held by men of other churches." This prophecy has been remarkably fulfilled. Not only did the centuries provide a continuous stream of travelers from all over the civilized world, but for many generations the bodies of princes, chiefs and kings

ISLE OF IONA

The Iona Community

Eilean Chaltha

The Well of Youth

Lagandorain

Village Strand of the Monks

Ridge of the Rees

Eilean Diin Ean

The Cathedral

Well of the North Wind

Dun I 332 ft

Foot of Il anornum

Temple Glen

Reilig Odhrain

Jetty

Fionn's Cell

Culbhuig Hill of the Querning

Hill of the Bannee

M'Lean's Cross

Village

Hill of Seaetty

Hill of the Queen's Little

Gull Lochine

Nunnery

Martyr's bay

Firth Moorland

Machine

Cow Oran

Street of the dead

Sand Eels bay

Hill of the Angels

Hill of the Queen

The Eminence

Ottess Cave

Meadow of the Monks

of the Monks

Spouting Cave

Dunguile Ridge

St Maartins Cave

Loch Staonaig

The Freight

Pigeons Cave

Columbus Bay

Marble Quarry

Cairn of the Back to Ireland

Port of the Coracle

were brought to Iona to lie in its hallowed soil.

Buchanan's "History of Scotland" gives the following record: "In the Abbey of Saint Columba, the bishops of the Isles fixed their residence, after their ancient seat in Eubonia was taken possession of by the English. Amidst the ruins there remains still a burying place or cemetery, common to all the noble families of the Western Islands, in which, conspicuous above the rest, stand three large tombs, at a little distance from each other; on these are placed sacred shrines turned toward the East, and on their Western sides are fixed small tables, with the inscriptions indicating to whom the tombs belong. That which is in the middle, has as its title, 'Tumulus Regum Scotiae' the Tomb of the Kings of Scotland, for there forty-eight kings of the Scots are said to have been buried. The one upon the right is inscribed, 'Tumulus Regum Hiberniae', the Tomb of the Kings of Ireland, where four Irish kings are reported to rest. And upon the one on the left is engraved, 'Tumulus Regum Norvegiae, the Tomb of the Kings of Norway', general rumour having assigned to it the ashes of eight Norwegian kings" (pg. 47).

On Iona, the "Stone Lia Fail" continued to be used as the Coronation Stone of the Dalriadic kings until its removal to Dunstaffnage, on the mainland of Scotland just east of Iona, where the Lords of Scotland were made princes. Tradition has it that the Clan Mac Dougall was made custodian of the Stone at Dunstaffnage till its removal to Scone Scotland.

There is an old tradition at Dunstaffnage to the effect that if a true descendant of the Mac Dougall's with red hair and without freckles should stand in the ancient chapel of Dunstaffnage and shout the battle cry of the Scots, "Strike for the Silver Lion", instead of an echo he will hear a ghostly voice say, "Where is the Stone?"

In 843 A.D., Kenneth Mac Alpin was crowned on the Stone Lia Fail as the first King of the United Kingdom of the Picts and the Scots. One of his first acts as King was to found a church at Scone (near Perth, Scotland) because it was there that he had gained his principal victory over the Picts. Kenneth then had the "Stone Lia Fail" brought from Dustaffnage and placed on an adjoining hill named "Moot Hill" or "Hill of Credulity." For centuries the Stone of Destiny was used as a Coronation Stone by the kings of Scotland. One of the earliest records of a coronation is preserved in the account of John of Fordun, the Scottish chronicler who died about A.D. 1384. He tells us that the Stone was used in the coronation of Alexander III in A.D. 1249:

"...and, having there placed him in the regal chair, decked with silk cloths and embroidered with gold, the Bishop of St. Andrew's, the others assisting him. consecrated his king, the king himself sitting, as was proper, upon the regal chair - that is, the Stone - and the earls and other nobles placing vestments under his feet with bent knees, before the Stone. This Stone is reverently preserved in that monastery for the consecration of kings of Scotland; nor were any of the kings in wont to reign anywhere in Scotland, unless they had, on receiving the name of king, first sat upon this royal Stone in Scone, which was constituted by ancient kings the 'sedes superior' or principal seat."

King Kenneth II (d. 995 A.D.) had the Stone placed on a wooden pedestal in front of the high altar of the Abbey of Scone. This pedestal had a wooden shaft which could be raised or lowered according the height of the monarch to be crowned, enabling the king to sit with comfort and dignity, his kilt being arranged to cover the Coronation Stone completely. At the same time, the King had an inscription engraved on one side of the Stone:

> Ni fallat fatum, Scoti quocunque
> Invenient lapidum regnare tenentur ibidem

Translation
> "If fate go right, where'er this Stone is found
> The Scots shall monarchs of that realm be crowned."

This prophecy was certainly fulfilled when King James VI of Scotland became James I of England. It should be noted that the present Royal House of Britain is descended from the Scottish kings, through Queen Elizabeth of Bohemia, the daughter of James VI, whose daughter Sophia married the Elector of Hanover; their son became Britain's King George I.

Another record relating to the kings of Scotland is found in the book, "Scots Coronations" by the Marquess of Bute which tells us that seven prayers were used at the ancient coronation of the Kings of Scotland. The following are extracts:

Prayer IV - "Lord, who from everlasting governest the kingdom of all kings, bless thou this ruling prince. Amen...And glorify him with such blessing that he may hold the sceptre of Salvation in the exaltation of David, and be found rich with the gifts of sanctifying mercy. Amen...Grant unto him by thine inspiration even to rule the people in meekness as thou didst cause Solomon to obtain a kingdom of peace. Amen."

Prayer V - "Almighty God give thee the dew of heaven and the fatness of the earth, and plenty of corn and wine. Let people serve thee and nations bow down to thee; be lord over thy brethren and let thy mother's sons bow down to thee. God shall be thine helper, and Almighty shall bless thee with blessings of heaven above, on the mountains and on the hills, blessings of the deep that lieth under, blessings of the beasts and of grapes and apples. The blessings of the ancient fathers, Abraham, and Isaac, and Jacob, be confirmed upon thee. Amen."

Prayer VI - "Bless, O Lord, the substance of our prince, and accept the work of his hands; and blessed of thee be his hand, for the precious things of heaven for the dew, and for the deep that coucheth beneath, and for the precious fruits brought forth by the sun and for the precious things put forth by the moon, and for the chief things of the ancient mountains, and for the precious things of the lasting hills, and fulness thereof; the blessing of Him that appeared in the bush come upon the head of (name); and let the blessing of the Lord be full upon his children; and let him dip his feet in oil, let his horns be like the horns of unicorns, with them shall he push the people together to the end of the earth, for let Him who rideth upon the heaven be his help for ever, Amen." (Pgs. 49-58).

The Marquess of Bute also quotes from a pamphlet entitled, "The Forme and Order of the Coronation of Charles, the Second, King of Scotland, England, France, and Ireland. As it was acted and done at Scone, the first day of January" (1651). It is the work of Sir James Balfour, the Lord Lyon King-of-Arms who officiated upon the occasion. The minister, who gave the sermon and exhortations from which the following extracts are taken, was the Rev. Robert Dowglas.

"When the King was set down upon the throne, the Minister spoke to him a word of exhortation: Sir, you are set down upon the throne in a very difficult time; I shall therefore put you in mind of a Scriptural expression of a Throne; it is said: 'Solomon sat on the Throne of the Lord', Sir, you are a king, and a king in covenant with the the Lord...It is the Lord's Throne, Remember that you have a King above you, the King of Kings, and Lord of Lords, who commandeth thrones...Your Throne is the Lord's Throne, and your people are the Lord's people. Let not your heart be lifted up above your brethren (Deut. 17:20). They are your brethren, not only of your flesh, but brethren by covenant with God...Your Throne is the Lords Throne. Beware of making His Throne a Throne of iniquity...But as the Throne is the Lord's Throne. let the laws be the Lord's laws, agreeable to His Word...Lastly, if your throne be the Throne of the Lord, take a word of encouragement against Throne adversaries. Your enemies are the enemies of the Lord's Throne" (Pgs. 191-201).

The ancient Abbey of Scone was destroyed in 1559 A.D. at the time of the Reformation. Today, that site is occupied by Scone Palace, the home of the Earls of Mansfield. On Moot Hill stands a stone chapel, marking the place where the Stone of Destiny had rested and where the kings of Scotland presided over their Parliaments until Edward I of England removed the Stone to Westminster Abbey in 1296 A.D.

Before the third overturning of the ancient relic, an event occurred that was most noteworthy. Its took place in Arbroath Abbey. Following the removal of the "Stone of Destiny" to Westminister, King Robert "the Bruce" of Scotland was visited by two emissaries of Pope John XXII to whom Edward II of England had appealed for help to compel Scotland to acknowledge England's lordship. These emissaries bore a message from the Pope advising Bruce to submit to Edward's claims, but Bruce and his nobles drafted a letter which they addressed to Pope John XXII and which can still be seen in the Register House in Edinburgh. It had attached to it coloured ribbons and seals with the signatures of Robert the Bruce and twenty-five of his nobles. The letter which is drafted April 6, 1320, reads in part:

"We know Most Holy Father and Lord, and from the chronicles and books of the ancients gather, that among other illustrious nations, our's, to wit, the nation of the Scots, has been distinguished by many honours; which passing from the greater Sythia through the Mediterranean Sea and Pillars of Hercules and sojourning in Spain among the most savage tribes through a long course of time, could nowhere be subjugated by any people however barbarous; and coming thence one thousand two hundred years after the outgoing of the People of Israel (Exodus), they by many victories and infinite toil, acquired for themselves the possessions in the West which they now hold...In their kingdom one hundred and thirteen kings of their own royal stock, no stranger intervening, have reigned..."

This letter thus asserts that the Scots who had the Stone were connected with the ancient people of Israel (the so-called Lost Tribes); whom archaeology has established became the Scythians and the Cimmerians of history, whose origin had been a mystery. Lost to their identity as foretold in the Scriptures, (Rom. 11:25), the Israelites migrated to their appointed land (IISam. 7:10); some crossing Europe by land, others by ships through the Mediterranean to the coast lands of Europe and the Isles in the West. The Scots claim ancestry to the branch of the Cimmerians (Celts) that dwelt in Spain for a period, and eventually came over to the Islands of Britain. They also claim that their royal line of kings (Zarah) has remained unbroken throughout their migrations.

THE SCOTTISH DECLARATION OF INDEPENDENCE

Josephus, the historian, writing in A.D. 70, seems to have had knowledge of the migrations of most of the Israelites from Asia toward Europe for, in his "Antiquities of the Jews" he writes: "...wherefore there are but two tribes in Asia and Europe subject to the Romans, while the ten tribes are beyond the Euphrates till now (A.D. 70) and are an immense multitude, and not to be estimated by numbers" (Book 11, chap. V).

"His glory is like the firstling of his bullock, and his horns are like the horns of unicorns: with them he shall push the people together to the ends of the earth: and they are the ten thousands of Ephraim, and they are the thousands of Manasseh" [Deut. 33:17].

51

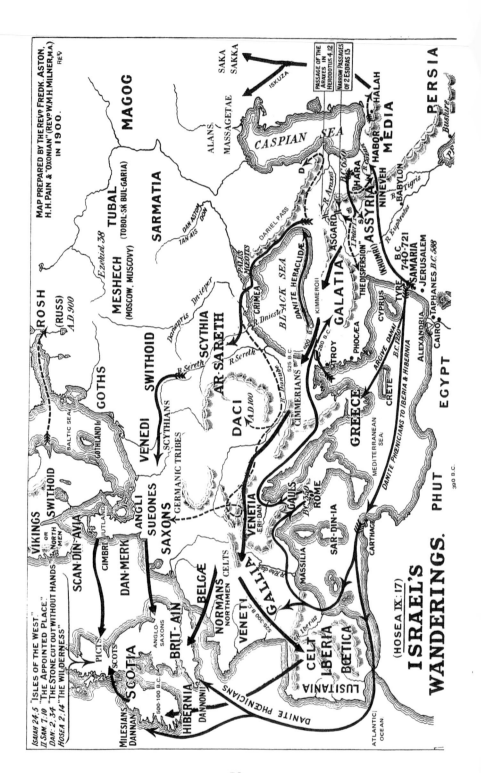

ISAIAH 24.5 "ISLES OF THE WEST."
II SAM. 7.10 "THE APPOINTED PLACE."
DAN. 2.34 "THE STONE CUT WITHOUT HANDS"
HOSEA 2.14 "THE WILDERNESS"

MAP PREPARED BY THE REV⁰ FREDK. ASTON,
H.H.PAIN & "OXONIAN" (REV⁰ W.M.H.MILNER,M.A.)
IN 1900.

(HOSEA IX:17)
ISRAEL'S WANDERINGS.

52

THE THIRD "OVERTURN"

The third "overturn" of Jacob's Bethel Stone was realized when Edward I of England (1296 A.D.) carried off the Stone to Westminster Abbey. There it became the crowning stone of the successors to the English throne. The common belief that the Stone of Scone was taken as spoil of war by Edward I, seems to be an error. The end of the 13th century saw the Scottish throne disputed by so many claimants that the Scots asked Edward I, noted for his wisdom, to arbitrate. He did so, on his terms that the Scots recognize him as "overlord". It is said that Edward noted the Scot's reverence for the "Stone of Scone". He was aware of the tradition inspired by the ancient inscription of King Kenneth II that wherever the Stone should be, a king of Gaelic blood would reign. Seeking to defeat this tradition, he had the Stone transferred to Westminster Abbey, where, ever since, it has been reverently cherished.

Not only was the Stone offered to Edward for safe-keeping but also the golden scepter, the crown of Scotland and some crown jewels. To show his respect for the Stone of Scone, Edward had built a beautiful chair of hardwood, six feet, seven inches high, in which to hold the Stone. Known as "Saint Edward's Chair" or the "Coronation Chair", it has ever since been kept in the Chapel named for him.

It was later claimed by the Scots, in connection with the Treaty of Northhampton, in 1328, that Edward II promised to restore the Stone to Robert the Bruce. The crown, scepter, emeralds, pearls, and rubies were returned. But the Stone was held in such respect by the people of London that they would not allow it to be removed. In spite of its location today, the ancient tradition that wherever the Stone should be, "a king of Gaelic blood would reign" has not failed. King James VI of Scotland was crowned on the Stone in Westminster Abbey when he became James I of England; and, today Britain's lovely Queen is Scottish.

Megahart's "Pillars of Hercules" gives the following Scottish account of the Coronation Stone removal to England:

"In Westminster Abbey there is a stone on which the kings of England are crowned. It was carried from Scone, where the kings of Scotland had been crowned upon it, and had been placed there by Kenneth, son of Alpen, after his victory over the Picts (in 843 A.D.). To Scone it had been transported from Dunstaffnage, where the successors of Fergus had been crowned upon it. To

Dunstaffnage it had been brought via Iona, from Tara, where the Scottish kings of Ireland had been crowned upon it, and Ireland had been named from it Innis Fail. To Tara it had been brought from Spain and to Spain, it was said, from the Holy Land...The importance attached to it was such as to make its removal to England to be considered, in the time of Edward I, a necessary step towards the subjugation of the Scottish Kingdom. They call it 'The Stone of Fortune', and the 'Stone of Destiny' (Lia Fail)."

ST. EDWARD'S CHAIR

The British Coronation Chair built around Jacob's stone which the Bible refers to as the Throne of God [i.e. set up by God].

John Harding, the English rhyming chronicler who wrote before A.D. 1465, says of Edward's removal of the Stone:

"And as he came home by Skoon away,
The regal there of Scotland than he brought,
And sent it forthe to Westmynstre for ay,
To ben ther ynne a chayer clenly wrought,
For masse prestes to sitte yn whan hem ought,
Whiche yit it there stondyng beside the shryne,
In a chaier of olde tyme made ful fyne".

Hollingshed's Chronicles gives this account: "When our king (Edward I) went forth to see the mountains, and understanding that all was a peace and quiet, he turned to the Abbey of Scone which was of chanons regular, where he took the stone, called the Regal of Scotland, upon which the kings of that nation were wont to sit at the time of their coronation for a throne, and sent it to the Abbey of Westminster. The Scots claim that this was the stone whereon Jacob slept when he fled into Mesopotamia".

From the time of King Edward I onward, all the Monarchs of England have been crowned on the "Stone of Destiny" and the Coronation Chair with the exception of Mary I (known as Bloody Mary). The present Queen Elizabeth II was crowned upon the Stone in 1953, in fulfillment of God's Covenant with David: "My covenant will I not break, nor alter the thing that is gone out of my lips. Once have I sworn by my holiness that I will not lie unto David, his seed shall endure for ever, and his throne as the sun before me. It shall be established for ever as the moon, and as a faithful witness in heaven. Selah" (Psalm 89:34-37).

Comparatively few Bible scholars are aware of the fact that the Monarchy of Britain as well as most of the other monarchies of Europe are descendant from Judah (recipient of the Sceptre promise - Gen. 49:10). In the Scottish National Library there is a Gaelic manuscript (by Dugald the Scot, son of McPhail, in A.D. 1467) containing the complete genealogies of the Scottish Kings, showing their descent through the Irish Kings by way of Judah, Jacob and Isaac back to Abraham. In Windsor Castle there is also a genealogical table showing the descent of the British kings from David through the Irish and Scottish lines. Thus the Monarchy existed long before there was a British Nation.

Whatever may be said of the story of Jacob's Pillar, as we have traced it, all will agree that it hangs together. While evidence for some links may not be strong, others are quite clear. God said plainly that He would "overturn, overturn, overturn" - "until He

(Shiloh, the Messiah) come whose right it is; and I will give it Him" (Ezek. 21:27). The Throne was "overturned" three times - from Jerusalem to Ireland; from Ireland to Scotland, and then from Scotland to England. This completed the three "overturnings." God's commission to the prophet Jeremiah "to pull down" the Throne of David and "to replant" it was accomplished.

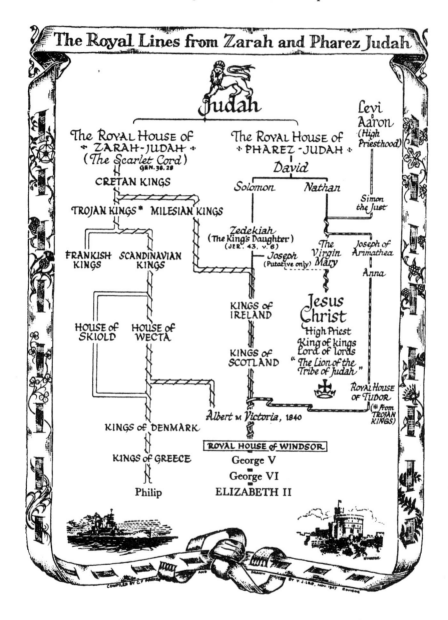

THE CORONATION STONE

The Coronation Stone that reposes in St. Edward's Chapel in Britain's sacred Abbey of Westminster has stirred men's imaginations for centuries. In light of Bible history no other inanimate object on earth has been given such honored use and glorious purpose as that given to this block of sandstone known as the "Stone of Destiny". What is its origin? What enshrines it with an importance far beyond its intrinsic value?

In his essay on "Certain Monuments of Antiquity", Weaver says (p. 118):

"It appears that the Irish kings, from very ancient times until A.D. 513, were crowned upon a particular sacred stone called 'Liath Fail', 'the Stone of Destiny', that, so also, were the Scottish kings until the year 1296, when Edward I of England brought it here. And it is a curious fact that this stone has not only remained in England unto now, and is existing still under the coronation chair of our British sovereigns in Westminster Abbey, but that all our kings, from James I, have been crowned in that chair. This being a fact so curious, we shall quote its particulars in a note taken from Toland, in his 'History of the Druids' (pp. 137-9)."

Toland's statement is this:

"The Fatal Stone (Liag Fail) so called, was the stone on which the supreme kings of Ireland used to be inaugurated, in time of heathenism on the hill of Tarah; it was superstitiously sent to confirm the Irish colony in the north of Great Britain, where it was continued as the coronation seat of the Scottish kings ever since Christianity; till in the year 1300 (1296 A.D.). Edward I, of England brought it from Scone, placing it under the coronation chair at Westminster, and there it still continues. I had almost forgot to tell you that it is now called by the vulgar, Jacob's stone - as if this had been Jacob's pillow at Bethel!".

Dean Stanley, one-time custodian of the Stone, in his book "Memorials of Westminster Abbey", sums up its historical importance in these words; "It is the one primevel monument which binds together the whole Empire. The iron rings, the battered surface, the crack which has all but rent its solid mass asunder, bear witness of the English monarchy - an element of poetic, patriarchal, heathen times, which, like Araunah's rocky threshing floor in the midst of the Temple of Solomon, carries back our thoughts to races and customs now almost extinct; a link which unites the Throne of England to the traditions of Tara and Iona" (2nd Edit. pg. 66).

In appearance the rugged surface of the Stone of Destiny is of a steely dull-purplish color, varying somewhat, and with some reddish veins. It is composed of calcareous sandstone and imbedded in it are a few pebbles; one of quartz and two others of a dark material (porhyrite or andesite?). Its shape is roughly "pillow-like" being about 26" in length; 16" in. width, and 10½" in depth. Across its surface runs a crack and some chisel-marks are still visible on one or two sides. It appears to have been in the process of being prepared for building purposes, but was discarded before being finished. There are two large iron rings (of some rust resistant alloy), one at each end of the Stone which hang loosely from eyes, made of similar metal let into the Stone.

The rings in the ends of the Stone would indicate that porter poles were once used to transport the Stone. At first, it would appear as if two poles were used, one of them passed through the ring at each end, so that four persons would be required to carry it. However, when turned up, these rings protrude above the top of the stone, enabling one pole to be passed through both rings across the top of the Stone, theoretically allowing it to be carried by only two persons.

In preparation for King George V's coronation, the Stone was temporarily removed from the Coronation Chair, and a photograph was taken of it. This photograph disclosed that a groove runs right across the stone from ring to ring. From its appearance this groove was not cut, but was clearly the result of friction from a single pole being passed across from ring to ring. Such an indentation and wearing away of material indicates the enormous amount of carrying that the Stone was subjected to. If, as it appears, a single pole was used, because of the weight of the Stone (about 336

58

pounds) it is probable that more than two persons actually carried the Stone. Yoke-like cross beams could have been attached to both ends of the pole for the convenience of two or more persons at each end of the pole.

British, Scotch and Irish records of the Stone of Destiny locate it at Tara, Ireland (some five centuries before Christ), from where it was transported to Scotland in circa A.D. 498 by Fergus the Great. From there it was taken to Iona circa A.D. 563; then to Dunstaffnage from where it was removed to Scone, near Perth, Scotland. Finally it was moved, by Edward I, to Westminster Abbey, London in A.D. 1296. Thus, from Tara to Westminster, covering over 1800 years of history, it was never carried to any appreciable extent. The mere removal from these places could not account for the wearing away of the Stone that was evidently caused by the friction of a pole used in constant carrying. This must have been the result of many months of continuous carrying, prior to its arrival in Tara. The story of its journeying from Bethel, in the time of Jacob, and its accompanying the children of Israel in the Wilderness, would account for its present condition.

One of the most significant facts about the Coronation Stone is that no similar rock formation exists in the British Isles. Professor Totten, the eminent professor of Science at Yale University, after making a thorough examination of the Stone made the following statement: "The analysis of the stone shows that there are absolutely no quarries in Scone or Iona where-from a block so constituted could possibly have come, nor yet from Tara". Professor Odlum, a geologist (and Professor of Theology at an Ontario University), also made microscopic examinations of the Coronation Stone, comparing it to similar stone from Scotland (including Iona and the quarries of Ireland) and found them dissimilar.

Professor Odlum became tremendously interested in the Stone. He was intrigued with the idea that perhaps its source could be found in Palestine, as suggested by the ancient records of Ireland. Determined to make the search, and after several weeks of unsuccessful exploration, Odlum discovered a stratum of sandstone near the Red Sea at Bethel, geologically the same as the Coronation Stone. Relating the circumstances of the discovery to a friend upon his return to Britain, the Professor stated:

"I put on my old mackintosh, I stuck my geologist's hammer in my pocket, and I went out for one last look. It was pouring rain. I walked along the same places I had walked over and over again, looking for stone. Suddenly, while I was walking along a certain pathway, with a rocky cliff on either side, the sun shone on the rain-streaked piece of rock, and I noticed a peculiar sort of glitter that I thought I recognized. I climbed up, and I found that wet rock, as far as I could see with the magnifying glass I had, was of the identical texture I had been looking for." I chipped off a piece from the living rock. I took it back to the hotel and examined it as well as I could. I was sure I had got what I wanted".

Although a microscopic test of the sample Bethel stone matched perfectly with the same test made of the Coronation Stone, the Professor wanted to make chemical tests of both stones. to dispel all doubts as to the source of Britain's treasured relic. To save time, Odlum cabled a geologist friend in England and said: "Will you do all you possibly can to get a piece of the Coronation Stone no bigger than a pea, in order that we may submit it to a chemical test." The geologist friend made application to the Dean of Westminster Abbey to be allowed to take a piece, no bigger than a pea, from the Coronation Stone. The Dean said: "I daren't let you have permission. The only way you can get permission would be from the Archbishop of Canterbury."

Application was made to the Archbishop of Canterbury, and this was the reply of the Archbishop: "To take a piece from that stone no bigger than a pea would require a special Act of Parliament to be passed by the House of Commons, endorsed by the House of Lords and signed by the King; and if you get that," said the Archbishop, "I won't give you permission."

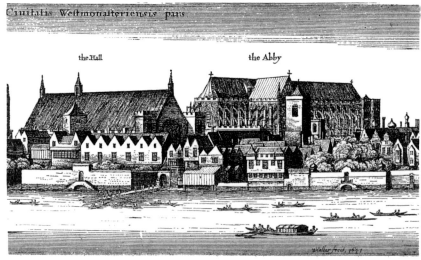

WESTMINSTER HALL AND ABBEY.

THEFT OF THE STONE

On Christmas Eve, 1950, the recesses of St. Edward's Chapel in Westminster Abby echoed to the sweet music of Noel. In the Chapel stood Britain's Coronation Chair, under it the Coronation Stone, standing just as they had stood for seven hundred years. In the silent, eerie dimness of the early hours of Christmas morning, furtive figures stealthily entered St. Edward's Chapel, then were gone – and so was the Coronation Stone.

How and by whom, this Stone, weghing over 300 pounds, was so surreptiously spirited from its resting-place, out of the locked Abbey, was once one of Britain's greatest mysteries. A splinter broken from the leg of the Coronation Chair, a short crowbar, some fingerprints, an unidentified wristwatch on the flagstones of the Abbey floor, marks on the altar step's carpet where the Stone had been dragged, and "J.F.S." carved on the chair itself were the only evidence of the "sacrilegious" crime which shocked all Britain. Naturally, the solving of such a crime became the first priority of Scotland Yard.

Despite the lack of evidence, it was believed that the Stone was stolen by persons having sympathy with the Scottish Nationalist movement. A week after the theft a letter was handed into the office of a Glasgow newspaper, the Daily Record, asking that one copy of the Petition accompanying the letter should go to the police and the other to the press. The Petition stated: "The petition of certain of his Majesty's most loyal and obedient subjects to his Majesty King George the Sixth humbly sheweth:

That his Majesty's petitioners are the persons who removed the Stone of Destiny from Westminster Abbey:

That, in removing the Stone of Destiny, they have no desire to injure his Majesty's property, nor to pay disrespect to the Church of which he is the temporal head:

That the Stone of Destiny is, however, the most ancient symbol of Scottish nationality and, having been removed from Scotland by force and retained in England in breach of the pledge of his Majesty's predecessor, King Edward III of England, and its proper place of retention is among his Majesty's Scottish people who, above all, hold this symbol dear:

That therefore his Majesty's petitioners will most readily return the stone to the safe keeping of his Majesty's officers if his Majesty will but graciously assure them that in all time coming the

Stone will remain in Scotland in such of his Majesty's properties or otherwise as shall be deemed fitting by him:

That such an assurance will in no way preclude the use of the Stone in any coronation of any of his Majesty's successors whether in England or Scotland:

That his Majesty's humble petitioners are prepared to submit to his Majesty's Ministers or their representatives proof that they are the people able, willing, and eager to restore the Stone of Destiny to the keeping of his Majesty's officers:

That his Majesty's petitioners, who have served him in peril and peace, pledge again their loyalty to him, saving always their right and duty to protest against the actions of his Ministers if such actions are contrary to the wishes of the spirit of his Majesty's people:

In witness of the good faith of his Majesty's petitioners the following information concerning a watch left in Westminster Abbey on December 25, 1950, is appended: (1) The mainspring of the watch was recently repaired; (2) The bar holding the right-hand wrist strap to the watch had recently been broken and soldered:

This information is given in lieu of signature by his Majesty's petitioners, being in fear of apprehension: "(Scottish Daily Express, Dec. 30, 1950).

There is an interesting story surrounding the actual taking of the Coronation Stone from Westminster Abbey and its escape to Scotland, which is offered as "hearsay". In pulling the Stone, by one of the iron rings (one embedded in each of the ends of the Stone), along the Abbey floor, an ancient crack in the Stone parted. The Stone of Destiny lay in two pieces. Its weight divided into two parts facilitated its removal from the Abbey.

Soon after the theft, an alarm was given and road-blocks were set up on all roads leading out of England, and everyone was asked to be on the look-out for the Stone - to report any suspicious circumstances. The car, with the Stone concealed as a cushion in the back seat with a coat covering it made a stop near the Scottish border for gasoline. When the occupants of the car were asked by the station attendant if they had the Stone of Destiny with them, they replied, "Aye sure, its in there, its in the boot". Letting the reward of over $2000.00 for information leading to the recovery of the Stone slip through his fingers the attendant laughing said, "Well, the police have been round once asking me what Scotsman

I've given petrol to. If they come back, I'll tell them the Stone went through this morning".

The Stone was subsequently repaired by doweling and cement. But, before sealing the two pieces together, a copy of the Scottish "Declaration of Independence" was placed between them. If true, then perhaps Scottish patriotism which naturally cries out for the Stone's restoration will be satisfied. Legally, the arguments in the "petition" are invalid. The Treaty of Northampton, referred to in the petition, was negotiated, not between England and Scotland, but between Edward, King of England and Robert, King of Scots. Since the rights of both later became vested in the same person, King George VI, the Sovereign of the United Kingdom, no transfer of title between them can make any difference today. The ownership of the Stone of Destiny is incontestable. It belongs to the heirs and descendants of King George VI who can trace his or her descent from both Edward III of England and Robert, King of the Scots.

Eventually the Stone of Destiny was recovered by the English. It was wrapped up in the Scottish flag (St. Andrew's Cross) and left upon the high altar of the ruined Abbey of Arbroath in Scotland, then the British authorities were notified of where it could be found. It was at Arbroath Abbey that King Robert the Bruce and the Scottish Barons drew up the famous "Declaration of Independence" which included the following:

"For so long as a hundred of us are left alive we will yield in no least way to English domination.We fight not for glory, nor for wealth nor for honour, but only and alone for freedom, which no good man surrenders but with his life".

ARBROATH ABBEY

THE CORONATION STONE

Photographed when removed from the Coronation Chair in preparation for the Coronation of George VI

THE CROWNING

The form of service used at the Coronation of the Kings and Queens of Britain can be traced back to the time of Egbert, Archbishop of York (A.D. 732-766), who was descended from the royal family of Northumbria. However, one cannot fail to be struck with the similarities between the coronation of Britain's rulers and that of the Kings of the House of David. Even the royal regalia would appear to have some connection with the power and position of the monarchs of ancient Israel. It cannot be pure coincidence that all the rituals of the coronation ceremony being used today are counterparts of those used in Old Testament days.

In the second book of Kings we read a striking account of the crowning of the King's son. The priest, whose name was "Jehoiada", sent and fetched the rulers and the captains of Israel and the guard (as done today), and he took an oath of them in the House of the Lord; *"And to the captains over hundreds did the priest give king David's spears and shields, that were in the temple of the Lord. And the guard stood, every man with his weapons in his hand, round about the king, from the right corner of the temple to the left corner of the temple, along by the altar and the temple. And he brought forth the king's son, and put the crown upon him, and gave him the testimony; and they made him king, and anointed him; and they clapped their hands, and said, God save the king"* (II Kings 11:10-12).

THE ENTRANCE OF THE KING INTO THE ABBEY

As the King and his Queen enter the great West Door of the Abbey they are met by the Civil and Ecclesiastical dignitaries who, bearing the Regalia, escort them up the Nave led by the choristers who sing the Anthem; "I was glad when they said unto me, we will go into the House of the Lord. (taken from the 122nd Psalm composed by King David). Our feet shall stand in thy gates, O Jerusalem. Jerusalem is built as a city that is at unity in itself." Other verses include "Whither the tribes go up...to give thanks unto...the Lord. For there are set...the thrones of the House of David. Pray for the peace of Jerusalem...Peace within thy walls, and prosperity within thy palaces".

THE PRESENTATION OF THE KING TO THE PEOPLE

At the East side and afterwards at the South, West and North sides the King is presented to the people, the Archbishop saying: "Sirs, I here present unto you King (name), your undoubted King: Wherefore all you who are come this day to do your homage and service, Are you willing to do the same? Each time the people signify their assent by acclamation, and cries of "GOD SAVE THE KING".

"And Samuel said to all the people, See ye him whom the Lord hath chosen that there is none like him among all the people? And all the people shouted, and said, God save the king" (I Sam. 10:24).

THE CORONATION SERMON

The Coronation sermon is delivered by either the Archbishop of Canterbury, or the Dean of the Abbey, or some prominent Churchman. The preaching of such a sermon absolutely originated in Israel. There are numerous examples of the Old Testament where the Prophet or Priest addressed the King and the people of Israel at their coronations. An examination of the sermons given at the crowning of various British Kings, shows that in nearly every instance the subjects of the addresses were based on Scriptures referring to the various Kings of Israel. A typical example is the sermon Bishop Drummond, preached at the Coronation of George III (1760) on I Kings 10:9, a Scripture addressed to King Solomon nearly 3000 years ago: *"Blessed be the Lord thy God, which delighted in thee, to set thee on the throne of Israel: because the Lord loved Israel for ever, therefore made he thee king, to do judgment and justice".*

THE CORONATION OATH

Following the sermon, the King expresses his free will to taking the oath and promises to uphold justice in the Kingdom. This he does by stating, "I am willing" and "All this will I do". He then goes to the Altar and placing his right hand on the Bible (God's Book of the Law) makes a solemn oath saying: "The things which I have before promised, I will perform and keep, so help me God". After kissing the open Book he reads aloud the following statement, he signs a copy of the same in ink with his royal signature:

66

"I do solemnly and sincerely, in the presence of God, profess, testify and declare, that I am a faithful member of the Protestant Reformed Church, by law established in England, and I will according to the true enactments which secure Protestant Succession to the throne of my Realm, uphold and maintain the said enactments, to the best of my powers, according to law".

"and Jehoiada (the high Priest) *made a covenant* (agreement) *between him, and between all the people, and between the king, that they should be the Lord's people"* (II Chron. 24:16).

THE ANOINTING

Anointing with oil was an act which God ordained long ago as an outward and visible sign of Divine election into an Office of special service. In I Kings 19:16 we read of Elijah being commanded of God to "Anoint Elisha to be a prophet". Again, at an earlier date, God commanded Moses to anoint Aaron..."that he may minister unto me in the priest's office" (Exod. 40:13-15). In the Coronation ceremony of the British kings, this ritual of anointing is still enacted, and is considered the "most important part of the service." As the King is seated in the Coronation Chair over the Coronation Stone (Stone of Destiny) the Archbishop of Canterbury reads the following prayer:

"O Lord, who by anointing with oil didst of old make and consecrate kings, priests, and prophets to teach and govern thy people Israel; bless and sanctify thy chosen servant (name), who by office and ministry is now to be anointed with this oil, and consecrated king of this realm: Strengthen him O Lord with the Holy Ghost the Comforter" At this moment the Choir begins singing the anthem "Zadoc, the Priest" by Handel, the words being taken from the account of Solomons' anointing by Zadoc, in B.C. 969 (I Kings 1:39,40).

Next, in order, comes the most sacred moment of the whole Coronation Ceremony, symbolising God's choice of the sovereign of the realm to sit on David's Throne. The Archbishop takes the

THE ANOINTING SPOON

The golden spoon in which the consecrated oil is poured; the handle is believed to have been made in the thirteenth century.

67

golden Spoon into which the Dean of the Abbey has poured some oil from the Ampulla or golden "Dove": from the Spoon, the

THE AMPULLA

The anointing oil is contained in this golden vessels, which is in the form of an eagle. It is part of the regalia which escaped destruction during the Cromwellian period.

The Ampulla, with the spoon, the most sacred objects in the regalia are also the oldest.

Archbishop anoints the king in the form of a cross, (1) on the head, saying, "Be thy head anointed with holy oil, as kings, priests and prophets were anointed"; (2) on the breast, saying, "Be anointed with holy oil"; (3) on the palms of both hands, saying, "Be thy hands anointed with holy oil; and as Solomon was anointed by Zadoc the priest and Nathan the prophet so be you anointed, blessed and consecrated king over this people whom the Lord your God hath given you to rule and govern, in the name of the Father, Son and Holy Ghost:".

"The king also said unto them, Take with you the servants of your lord, and cause Solomon my son to ride upon my own mule, and bring him down to Gihon: And let Zadoc the priest and Nathan the prophet anoint him there king over Israel: and blow ye with the trumpet (this is also done today), *and say, God save king Solomon"* (I Kings 1: 33, 34).

"And Zadok the priest took an horn of oil out of the tabernacle, and anointed Solomon. And they blew the trumpet: and all the people said, God save king Solomon" (I Kings 1:39).

THE PRESENTING OF THE SPURS AND SWORD

After the anointing of the King there follows the delivery of the royal regalia: The touching with the Spurs, emblem of chivalry, and the girding of the Swords (the Pointed Sword of Spiritual Justice or "Sword of State" and the Curtana, or Unpointed "Sword of Mercy"), together with the offering of the same upon the Altar, signify the King's intent, under God, to rule in justice, equity and mercy.

ST. GEORGE'S SPURS

The golden spurs, which the Queen touches, are emblems of knightly chivalry. At one time they were worn at the Ceremony.

THE KING'S SWORD OF STATE AND SWORD OF MERCY.

"Thus speaketh the Lord of hosts, saying, Execute true judgment, and shew mercy, and compassions every man to his brother: And oppress not the widow, nor the fatherless, the stranger, nor the poor; and let none of you imagine evil against his brother in your heart" (Zech. 7:9, 10).

THE PRESENTING OF THE BRACELETS

A minor but a very significant part. of the ceremony is the presentation of the Bracelets to the King. This designates the military factor, representing the King as the one called to lead and encourage his people and his armies in the defense of the realm against all outside aggression. If we turn to the Scriptures we find this custom also comes from the earliest days of Israel, at the time when David was first made king after the death of King Saul. The Amalekite who, at King Saul's request, stood over him and slew him, brought tidings to David of the death of Saul and Jonathan, and said to David: *"So I stood upon him, and slew him, because I was sure that he could not live after that he was fallen: and I took the crown that was upon his head, and the bracelet that was on his arm, and have brought them hither unto my lord"* (II Sam. 1:10).

THE BRACELETS

An emblem of Royalty dating back to most ancient times. The Bracelets of Sincerity were made for Charles II.

THE PRESENTING OF THE ROBE AND ORB

The next event in the Coronation Service is the investiture of the King with the Imperial Robe. At the same time, he is given the Orb (a golden sphere six inches in diameter), surmounted by the Cross. The King arises as the Dean of Westminister places the priestly garments upon him (the "Colobium Sindonis" and the "Supertunica" or close pall of cloth-of-gold, together with a Girdle of the same). The Dean then takes the Orb with the Cross from the Altar and places it in the hands of the Archbishop who, in turn, delivers it into the hands of the King. The Archbishop then says:

"Receive this Imperial Robe and Orb; and the Lord your God endue you with knowledge and wisdom, with majesty and with power from on high. The Lord clothe you with the 'Robe of righteousness' and with the Garment of salvation. And when you see this orb set under the Cross, remember that the whole world is subject to the power and Empire of Christ our Redeemer. For He is the Prince of the kings of the earth; King of Kings and Lord of Lords, so that no man can reign happily who derives not his authority from Him, and directs not all his actions according to His Laws".

THE ORB

A golden ball surmounted by a Cross symbolizes the sovereignty of Christianity over the world.

The "Colobium Sindonis", or under-tunic indicates that the King is the Head of the Church and symbolizes his Majesty's priestly functions and represents our Lord's clothes after they had cast lots for His garments at the Crucifixion. This investiture of the Imperial Robe is also an ancient custom. It formed part of the Irish coronation on the Stone of Destiny in 582 B.C., but its first appearance was in the Wilderness at Sinai after the Exodus. *"And these are the garments which they shall make; a breastplate, and an ephod, and a robe, and a broidered coat, a mitre, and a girdle: and they shall make holy garments for Aaron thy brother, and his sons, that he may minster unto me in the priests office"* (Exodus 28:4).

THE PRESENTING OF THE RING

The Coronation Ring which is now placed upon the fourth finger of the King's right hand, is often referred to as the "Wedding Ring" of England. The Ring signifies the union of the King with his people; his marriage to the nation. The symbolism of this rite has a Biblical parallel. According to the Biblical record, the Lord Jehovah was "married" to the Nation of Israel: *"Turn, O backsliding children, saith the Lord; for I am married unto you"* (Jer. 3:14).

71

In ancient times the Ring was a symbol of power and honor, as the following references reveal: *"And Pharaoh, took off his ring from his hand, and put it upon Joseph's hand"* (Gen. 41:42). *"But the father said to his servants, Bring forth the best robe, and put it on him; and put a ring on his hand"* (Luke 15:22).

THE CORONATION RING

The ring with which the Sovereign is wedded to the State.

THE PRESENTING OF THE SCEPTRE AND THE ROD

The next step is the presentation of two Rods to the King. Both rods have a small Orb (the World) surmounting them at the top. One is mounted with a cross above the Orb and is called the "Sceptre" which is held in the King's right hand. The other is mounted with a dove and is simply called the "Rod". The official report of this part of the ceremony is given as follows:

"The Sceptre with the cross is given into the right hand, as the emblem of kingly power, while in his left hand is placed the Rod with the dove symbolising equity and mercy".

THE ROYAL SCEPTRE

with the Dove, symbolic of the Holy Ghost, is held in the Sovereign's left hand.

THE ROYAL SCEPTRE

with the Cross is held in the Sovereign's right hand. It contains the magnificent diamond 'Star of Africa'.

The institution of the Sceptre and Rod as the emblems of authority for the Kings or High Priests, goes right back to the adoption of the Israel nation (as distinct from Jewry) as God's Kingdom upon the earth. In the days of the Exodus from Egypt in 1453 B.C., God formed Israel into a Kingdom under a code of statutes and laws, with Himself as King. At the same time God appointed two men Moses and his brother Aaron, to wield the Sceptre and the Rod, as they led Israel from Egypt to Palestine.

Moses wielded the Sceptre as Israel's uncrowned King, the Vice-Regent of God, their eternal King. From the time that God called him, Moses used the Sceptre or Rod as evidence that he was the Captain of Israel. In their flight from Egypt, when the children of Israel came face to face with the Red Sea, with the Egyptian chariots hotly pursuing them, we read in Exodus 14: 15,16, that *"The Lord said unto Moses...speak unto the children that they go forward; But lift up thy rod, and stretch out thine hand over the sea, and divide it: and the children of Israel shall go on dry ground through the midst of the sea"*. (Four hundred years later, when the throne of David was established over Israel, her Kings wielded the Sceptre as the emblem of their Kingly office).

As to Moses' brother Aaron, he was chosen to be the one who would supervise the religious life of Israel which was centered in the services held in the Tabernacle and in Solomon's Temple. The manifestations of Aaron's God-given authority was also by means of a Rod. The Old Testament books of Exodus and Numbers repeatedly narrate incidents where Aaron used his Rod in the manner God directed him, to fulfill his office of High-Priest.

These divided offices, however, were never intended to remain in perpetuity, and when the New Testament or New Covenant came in, a new order had to be introduced, combining King and Priest in one. The Scriptures make it very clear that Jesus Christ came from the line of Judah, not from the priestly tribe of Levi. Before the advent of Jesus a person from the Judah line could not stand as Israel's High Priest, but when Christ was crucified there occurred a great change in Israel's Ordinances. We read that at that time, by an unseen hand, the *"Veil of the temple was rent in twain from the top to the bottom"* (Matt. 27:51).

This act designated the closing of the old ordinances and priesthood. The new "Great High Priest", by His own crucifixion and death as the slain "Lamb", had put an end for ever to the Old Testament dispensation and order, *"blotting out the handwriting of ordinances that was against us, which was contrary to us, and took it out of the way, nailing it to his cross"* (Colossians 2:14).

.It should be noted that it was the "Ecclesiastical Law" containing the Ordinances (Eph. 2:15), administered by the House of Aaron that were "nailed to the cross", whereas the National Law, containing the commandments, statutes and judgments (Deut. 4:1; 5:31; 7:11; 26:46; Lev. 26:46) administrated by the House of David was "ratified" by Christ (Matt. 5:17; Dan. 9:25). These are operative today.

When Christ arose from the tomb He became the initiator of a New Covenant order; the new order in which the offices of King and Priest were to be combined in one person. This is referred to, in the Epistle to the Hebrews, as "the order of Melchisedec" (Heb. 7:10-17). In Genesis Melchisedek is called both "king" and "priest" (Gen 14:18). Christ was made "a priest for ever after the order of Melchisedec" (Heb. 5: 6), *"Who needeth not daily, as those high priests, to offer up sacrifice, first for his own sins, and then for the people's: for this he did once, when he offered up himself"* (Heb. 7: 27).

Once we understand the symbolism of Jacob's Pillar as representing both the House of God and the Throne of David, and accept the fact that God's Covenant with David is in effect, then the significance of both the Rod and the Sceptre being put into the hands of one person (a descendant of David as is the case with the present monarchy of Britain) is seen. It foreshadows the fact that our Great High Priest crowned "King of Israel" will eventually lead all men and nations, tribes, languages, and peoples, into His ultimate world-wide dominion of peace and justice.

Concluding the ceremony of the Archbishop's presentation of Sceptre and Rod to the King, the following exhortation is given: "God, from Whom all holy desire, all good counsels, and all just works do proceed, direct and assist you in the administration and exercise of all those powers which he hath given you. Be so merciful that you be not too remiss; so execute justice that you forget not mercy. Judge with righteousness, and reprove with equity, and accept no man's person. Abase the proud, and lift up the lowly; punish the wicked, protect and cherish the just, and lead your people into the way they should go: thus in all things follow His great and holy example, of whom the prophet David said, "Thou lovest righteousness, and hatest iniquity: the Sceptre of thy Kingdom is righteousness', even Jesus Christ our Lord" (paraphrase of Psa. 45: 6, 7).

THE PUTTING ON OF THE CROWN

After having been invested with the emblems and insignia of royal dignity, the King (seated over the Stone of Destiny) receives the Crown. This act is the great climax of the Coronation Ceremony and formally expresses the common tie between all the subjects of the Empire. This unity is manifested in the personality of the Sovereign. In other words, "the symbol and the bond of British unity are not in the flag, an institution, or a constitution, but the occupant of the Throne" (Governments of the British Empire by Prof. Barridale Keith).

ST. EDWARD'S CROWN

The Crown which is used for the act of Crowning, and worn for a short while during the Ceremony. The two arches signify Hereditary and Independent Monarchy, and are depressed at the centre to indicate a royal, not an imperial, crown.

The Royal Crown (or Crown of England) is also known as St. Edward's Crown, because it is a copy of the one used by King Edward the Confessor (founder of Westminister Abbey). The original crown was destroyed with most of the Royal Regalia during the brief period of the Commonwealth. There are several interesting and highly significant points in the design of the Crown:

First: At the summit of the whole design, even above the Crown itself, stands the Cross, the Cross of Jesus Christ. The King, in accepting this Crown, acknowledges his allegiance to, and the supremacy of, the Lord Jesus Christ.

Second: The rim or circlet of the Crown is set with twelve large stones of various colors each surrounded by diamonds. The number and the coloring of the twelve stones are most significant. They are identical with those which God commanded Israel's High Priest to wear throughout her history as a Kingdom-nation.

THE BREASTPLATE WITH ITS TWELVE JEWELS.

If we go back to the earliest days of God's Kingdom-nation at Sinai, we find God commanded that Israel's High Priest should wear a "Breastplate" of pure gold set with twelve precious stones. The number (representing the 12 tribes) and colors of those stones is most significant, being reflected in the national colors of Britain (Red, White and Blue) and the Royal Purple and Gold. These were outstanding colors within the Tabernacle in the Wilderness. God said to Moses:

"Thou shalt make a breastplate of judgment with cunning work; after the work of the ephod thou shalt make it; of gold, of blue and of purple, and of scarlet, and of fine twined linen (white) *shalt thou make it...And thou shalt set it in settings of stones, even four rows of stones: the first row shall be sardius, a topaz, and a carbuncle: this shall be the first row. And the second row shall be an emerald, a sapphire, and a diamond. And the third row a ligure,*

76

an agate, and an amethyst. *And the fourth row a beryl, and an onyx, and a jasper: they shall be set in gold in their inclosings. And the stones shall be with the names of the children of Israel, twelve, according to their names, like the engravings of a signet; every one with his name shall they be according to the twelve tribes"* (Exodus 28:15-21).

The King in wearing the Crown of twelve stones is literally the "high priest" or head of the Church of the Nation and as such foreshadows the day of redemption, deliverance and kingship spoken of by the prophet Zechariah who wrote: *"And the Lord their God shall save them in that day as the flock of his people: for they shall be as the stones of a crown, lifted up as an ensign upon his land. For how great is his goodness, and how great is his beauty!*(Zech. 9: 16, 17).

When the Crown is placed upon the King's head, the Archbishop prays to the original Jehovah, King of the Israel Kingdom-Race, saying: "O God, who crownest thy faithful Servant with mercy and loving kindness; look down upon this thy servant (name) our King, who now in lowly devotion boweth his head to thy Divine Majesty; and as thou dost this day set a Crown of pure gold upon his head, so enrich his royal heart with thy heavenly grace, and crown him with all princely virtues which may adorn the high station wherein thou hast placed him, through Jesus Christ Our Lord, to whom be honor and glory for ever".

IMPERIAL CROWN

After the Homage the King exchanges the St. Edwards Crown for the Imperial Crown of State which is worn on the return journey to Buckingham Palace.

After the Crowning, the King is presented with a purple-velvet-bound Holy Bible from the Altar. This custom originated at the Coronation Ceremony of William and Mary, who were Protestants. Today, as then, the Archbishop places the Bible in the hands of the King saying: "Our gracious King, we present you with this Book, the most valuable thing that this world affords. Here is wisdom. This is the royal law. These are the lively Oracles of God".

Such presentations of His own living Word was the command of God to His Kingdom People over 5000 years ago, for God said to His servant Moses: *"When thou are come unto the land which the Lord thy God giveth thee, and shalt possess it, and shalt dwell therein, and shalt say, I will set a king over me, like as all the nations that are about me...And it shall be, when he sitteth upon the throne of his kingdom, that he shall write him a copy of this law in a book out of that which is before the priests the Levites: And it shall be with him, and he shall read therein all the days of his life: that he may learn to fear the Lord his God, to keep all the words of this law and these statutes to do them"* (Deut. 17:14-19).

As the Crowning nears its completion a further acknowledgement of Divine Providence is given by the choir who sings the following Anthem, inspired by the words of David's Psalm 21:1-3:

"The king shall rejoice in thy strength O Lord.
Exceeding glad shall he be of thy salvation.
Thou hast presented him with the blessings of goodness
Thou hast set a Crown of pure gold upon his head."

THE ACCLAMATION

At the completion of the Crowning, the whole congregation of the people, accompanied by loud and joyous blowing of the trumpets, give voice to their recognition of the rightful choice of the King by shouting loudly and repeatedly, "GOD SAVE THE KING!" Once more we are reminded of the deep spiritual significance of this ceremony. It is a hallowing, a dedication, a setting apart and a repetition of the Children of Israel expressing their pleasure and approval in joyous acclamation at the coronation of their Kings: *"And all the people came up after him, and the people piped with pipes, and rejoiced with great joy, so that the earth rent with the sound of them"* (I Kings 1:40) *"And when she looked, behold, the king stood by a pillar, as the manner was, and the princes and the trumpeters by the king, and all the people of the land rejoiced, and blew with trumpets"* (II Kings 11:14).

Finally, His Majesty, the King, anointed, crowned and vested with all the titles and insignia of Royal power and dignity, leaves the Westminster Abbey in solemn procession, and passes into the streets of the city to receive the plaudits of the people.

GOD AND MY [BIRTH] RIGHT

THE CORONATION OF QUEEN ELIZABETH II JUNE 2, 1953

Her Majesty, wearing St. Edward's Crown and seated on the Throne, receives the homage of her bishops during the Coronation ceremony in Westminster Abbey.

79

THE EVERLASTING THRONE OF DAVID

The history of Jacob's Pillar and the Throne of David reveals a fantastic story, fascinating as it is significant; a story that not only epitomizes the history of Ireland, Scotland and England, but offers an astonishing revelation pertaining to the "Ten Lost Tribes" of Israel. Its plot line centers about the destiny of the Anglo-Saxon peoples, in fact, of the entire English-speaking world together with those Western European nations culturally and spiritually identified with it. In the entire history of mankind no other "stone" or racial symbol has been so long possessed by the descendants of its original owners. Since it first came into historic notice, it has occupied an exalted place. It would be difficult to portray the eventual greatness of that position (to) which prophecy speaks.

Down through the ages man's symbols became enlarged in their importance from mere representations of visualized things to symbolizing ideas, ideals, standards, guilds, institutions, creeds and ideologies. These symbols became signs of beliefs, faiths, covenants and creeds for which men have lived, fought and died. Throughout the ages peoples, especially oppressed peoples, have demanded leaders who could give them a "sign" which would free them from slavery and death and lead them out of the wilderness of oppression. That sign might be a "cloud by day", "a pillar of fire by night", a cross or a crescent, a symbol on a banner or a battle shield.

The power of a symbol was not in the symbol itself, but in man's faith in the intangible property it represented, and in the interpretation he gave it. So, for this Stone of Destiny, its power lies in the significance of the interpretation given by those for whom it has meaning.

Returning to the prophecy of Ezekial with regards to the "overturnings", we note that there were to be three overturns, but no more, UNTIL he comes whose right it is. In other words, the crown and the throne of David were transferred (as we found) to the Branch of the Scarlet Thread, to remain there until a certain time when some important person shall come, who has a right to the throne and crown. Who is "he" whose right it is? There can be only one person to whom rightfully belongs the crown and throne of David, and that is God Himself in the person of Jesus Christ: *"He* (Jesus) *shall be great, and shall be CALLED the Son of the Highest: and the Lord God shall give unto Him the throne of his father David: And he shall reign over the house of Jacob for ever; and of his KINGDOM there shall be no end"* (Luke 1: 32,33). When

"He" receives that throne and crown, however, another "overturn" is implied. It will mean the end of the Branch of the Scarlet Thread. The "breach" in the line of Pharez will be passed, and the rightful claimant to the throne will be restored.

In Zechariah we have the prophetic promise of a coming day of triumph for this "Stone" when it is brought forth in the coming greatest of all coronations when Jesus Christ shall take over the Throne of His earth father, David, and reign over the Stone Kingdom, or House of Jacob, forever: *"Who art thou O great mountain? before Zerubbabel thou shalt become a plain: and he shall bring forth the headstone thereof with shoutings crying, Grace, grace, unto it"* (Zech. 4:7).

It is difficult at times to tell (in the Scriptures) whether the Bethel Stone is being used as the emblem solely of Christ, or of His Kingdom, or of both. Paul declared that the Rock which went with Israel was Christ and Isaiah tells us: *"Therefore this saith the Lord God, Behold, I lay in Zion for a foundation a stone, a tried stone, a precious corner stone, a sure foundation: he that believeth shall not make haste. Judgment also will I lay to the line, and righteousness to the plummet"* (Isa. 28: 16,17). The importance of this same "stone" is also indicated in the following quotation from Psalms: *"The stone which the builders refused is become the head stone of the corner. This is the Lord's doing; it is marvellous in our eyes"* (Psalm 28: 22, 23).

In Matthew, our Lord blends the meaning of the "stone" with Himself and the Kingdom: *"Jesus said unto them, Did ye never read the scriptures, The stone which the builders rejected, the same is become the head of the corner: this is the Lord's doing, and it is marvellous in our eyes? Therefore say I unto you, the kingdom of God shall be taken from you and given to a NATION bringing forth the fruits thereof. And whosoever shall fall on this stone shall be broken: but on whomsoever it shall fall, it will grind him to powder"* (Matt. 21:42-44). It is this grinding process that Daniel tells us the "Stone Kingdom" would accomplish, when it falls upon the Kingdoms represented by the gold, silver, brass, iron and clay image (Dan. 2:31-35).

Long ago, God selected a people (through Abraham) to fulfill His purpose in the earth; to become a *"great nation"* and a *"a company of nations"* and to establish righteous governments. Through sin, a disobedience to the laws of God, they became *"blind to their identity"* and were chastised by captivity to become *"wanders among the nations"* (Hosea 9:17). Within a small

82

remnant of Israel, the Davidic Throne line was carried through the Irish, Scottish nations to ultimately rest in England.

Today, Britain has the honor and blessing of being custodians of Jacob's Pillar and maintaining the continuity of David's Throne. In this way, they fulfill God's covenant with David *"Once I have sworn by my holiness that I will not lie unto David. His seed shall endure forever, and his throne as the sun before me. It shall be established for ever as the moon, and as a faithful witness in heaven"* (Psalm 89:35-37).

"For thus saith the Lord; David shall never want a man to sit upon the throne of the house of Israel" (Jer. 33:17). *"Thus saith the Lord; If ye can break my covenant of the day, and my covenant of the night, and that there should not be day and night in their season; Then may also my covenant be broken with David my servant, that he should not have a son to reign upon his throne"* (Jer. 33: 20,21).

One need not worry to much about the geographical location of the Stone. Through the ages, Jacob's Pillar seems to have fulfilled its Divine purpose and the prophecy of Israel. Perhaps we are reaching the time when the "Old Order" passeth, and a Divine "New Order" shall be established. There was a time, nearly three thousand years ago, when the original nation of Israel were the recipients of abundance peace, health, wealth and happiness. This was the result of walking in obedience to God's Laws under the leadership of King Solomon, a "man of peace" — it was Israel's "Golden Age".

God not only confirms the perpetuity of the Throne of David (over some portion of Israel) by referring to the ordinances of heaven but also the continuity of the nation of Israel in the same way: *"Thus saith the Lord, which giveth the sun for a light by day, and the ordinances of the moon and of the stars for a light by night, which divided the sea when the waves thereon roar; The Lord of Hosts is his name: If those ordinances depart from before me, saith the Lord, then the seed of Israel also shall cease from being a nation before me for ever"* (Jer. 31:35, 36).

THE LORD'S PRAYER

If any be distressed, and fain would gather
Some comfort, let him hast unto

OUR FATHER

For we of hope and help are quite bereaven,
Except Thou succour us,

WHO ART IN HEAVEN

Thou shewest mercy, therefore for the same,
We praise Thee, singing

HALLOWED BE THY NAME

Of all our miseries cast up the sum
Show us Thy joys, and let

THY KINGDOM COME

We mortal are, and alter from our birth
Thou constant art,

THY WILL BE DONE ON EARTH

Thou mad'st the earth as well as planets seven
Thy Name be blessed here,

AS 'TIS IN HEAVEN.

Nothing we have to use, or debts to pay,
Except Thou give it us,

GIVE US THIS DAY

Wherewith to clothe us, wherewith to be fed,
For without Thee we want

OUR DAILY BREAD.

We want, but want no faults, for no day passes
But we do sin;

FORGIVE US OUR TRESPASSES

No man from sinning ever free did live,
Forgive us, Lord, our sins

AS WE FORGIVE

If we repent our faults, Thou ne'er disdaineth us:
We pardon them

THAT TRESPASS AGAINST US.

Forgive us that is past, a new path tread us,
Direct us always in Thy Faith,

AND LEAD US

We, thine own people and Thy chosen nation,
Into all truth, but

NOT INTO TEMPTATION.

Thou that of all good graces art the Giver,
Suffer us not to wander

BUT DELIVER

Us from the fierce assaults of world and devil,
And flesh, so shalt Thou free us

FROM ALL EVIL.

To these petitions let both Church and laymen
With one consent of heart and voice, say   AMEN.

THY KINGDOM COME

Many Bible students today, fail to recognize the Kingdom of God (called the Kingdom of Heaven by Matthew) to be a literal kingdom. However, on the authority of the angel Gabriel (Luke 1:32,33) we have to concede Jesus was destined from and before His birth to occupy a literal throne and reign over a literal kingdom. Unless such a kingdom eventuates and unless Jesus ascends the throne of that kingdom the words of the angel must be dismissed as false and misleading. If such an hypothesis could be maintained the whole fabric of the Christian religion would collapse.

Jesus taught His disciples to pray *"Thy kingdom come"*. The form of that petition is significant and introduces us to a phase of the question that is of the utmost importance. Obviously the Kingdom had not come when He issued the command. Had the Kingdom "come" then there would have been no need to pray for its coming. We continue to pray that same prayer. It follows that the Kingdom has not yet come, for if the Kingdom has come, whether under the title Kingdom or under any other title, our prayer becomes a meaningless exercise.

The word "come" (as used in the prayer) calls for careful understanding. Webster's "International Dictionary" gives six different uses of the word "come".

1. To move hitherward; to draw near; to approach the speaker...opposed to go.

2. To complete a movement toward a place; to arrive.

3. To approach or arrive, as if by a jouney or from a distance.

4. To approach or arrive, as the result of a cause, or the act of another.

5. To arrive in sight, to be manifest; to appear.

6. To get to be, as the result of change or progress.

There is one common element in all these definitions of the word "come". The person, thing, or quality that comes, or is to come, is already in existence when the "coming" begins. We must conclude, therefore, that the Kingdom can "come" only because it already exists. It is conceivable that a thing may begin to exist only a fraction of time before its movement begins. But we cannot postulate such an interval for the Kingdom, for Jesus is directing His followers to pray for the coming of the Kingdom of the Father and of that Kingdom it is said: *"Thy kingdom is an everlasting kingdom, and thy dominion endureth throughout all generations"*

(Psalm 145:13). The kingdom is therefore definitely the Kingdom of God.

The existence of the Kingdom of God was fundamental to the thought and teaching of Jesus. He began His ministry and ended His life on earth with the word Kingdom on His lips. According to St. Matthew, His first public utterance was *"Repent: for the Kingdom of Heaven is at hand"*(Matt. 4:17). According to St. Mark *"Jesus came into Galilee, preaching the Gospel of the Kingdom of God"* (Mark 1:14). According to St. Luke, in His various manifestations to His friends between His resurrection and Ascension, His constant theme was the Kingdom of God, and before He departed from them into Heaven His last word was about the Kingdom (Act 1:1-8).

Nearly all of the Parables of Jesus make explicit reference to the Kingdom idea. There seems no justification for this multiplicity of similes unless Jesus intended to stress the importance of the coming Kingdom in His scheme of things. Eleven of the Parables begin, *"the Kingdom of Heaven is like"*:

1. A man sowing seed . . . . .Matt. 13:3

2. A grain of mustard seed . . . . .Matt. 13:31

3. Leaven which a woman put into meal . . . . .Matt. 13:33

4. A treasure hid in a field. . . . . .Matt. 13:44

5. A merchant seeking goodly pearls . . . . .Matt 13:45

6. A net cast into the sea. . . . . .Mat. 13:47

7. A King who took account of his servants . . . . . . .Matt. 18:23

8. A householder hiring workers in his vineyard . . .Matt. 20:1

10. Ten virgins at a wedding .Matt. 25:1

11. A man travelling into a far country . . . . .Matt. 25:14

9. A King making a marriage feast for his son . . . . . .Matt. 22:2

Luke records Jesus speaking of the Kingdom of God as "within you" (margin gives "among you") (Luke 17: 20,21). There has been much discussion on the precise meaning of the Greek preposition "entos" which occurs only twice in the New Testament. The Revised Version retains "within you" in the text but gives a marginal note "or, in the midst of you". Moffat gives "in your midst". Alford's Greek Testament definitely adopts the word "among" as a true translation of "entos", and says: "The misunderstanding which renders these words "within you"

86

meaning this in a spiritual sense, 'in your hearts', should have been prevented by reflecting that they are addressed to the Pharisees, in whose hearts it certainly was not. Nor could the expression in this connection bear well this spiritual meaning potentially i.e. in its nature within your hearts.

It should be noted that despite the continuous conflict between Jesus and the Pharisees as a class, there were many individual Pharisees among the "good seed", children of the Kingdom (Parable of the Sower). *"And one of the Pharisees desired that he would eat with him. And he went unto the Pharisee's house, and sat down to meat"* (Luke 7:36). *"And it came to pass, as he went into the house of one of the chief Pharisees to eat bread on the sabbath day, that they watched him"* (Luke 14:1). From these and other incidents we must conclude that whatever antipathy existed between Jesus and the Pharisees as a whole, there were individual Pharisees who regarded Him with favour and with whom He held friendly relations.

Some scholars have suggested that since Jesus Himself and His disciples were among the Pharisees at the time it was literally true that the Kingdom of God was among them, but that might be dismissed as a verbal expedient. It is conceivable that "within" could mean "within their ranks", however, the expression "The Kingdom of God is among you" seems to fit all the requirements much better than "the Kingdom of God is within you".

To paraphrase the words of Luke: "The Kingdom of God is coming, but you will not perceive it, for your eyes are blinded. The Kingdom is coming, but men will not be able to locate it, for it is hidden. In fact it is here among you today, but you do not observe or understand. It comes in secret, unseen by you, and yet all the time it is in the midst of you" (Luke 17: 20, 21) .

"But in the last days it shall come to pass, that the mountain [government] of the house of the Lord shall be established in the top of the mountains (all governments), and it shall be exalted above the hills (all authorities); and people shall flow unto it. And many nations shall come, and say, Come, and let us go up to the mountain (government) of the Lord, and to the house of the God of Jacob; and he will teach us of his ways, and we will walk in his paths: for the law shall go forth of Zion, and the word of the Lord of Jerusalem" (Micah 4:1, 2).

When Jesus Christ returns to take the earthly Throne of David and to be established as King in His Kingdom then those called to reign with Him will begin the great work of the

Millenium. In the days of the Old Covenant, the Wilderness Tabernacle foreshadowed the order of those who will be called to administer the Kingdom. A very small company (symbolized by Aaron and his sons who received the "holy anointing oil"), the little flock of overcomers, entering the Tabernacle (the "Body of Christ") to reign with Him. A larger company (symbolized by the Levites who were called of God for national service but not "anointed") called to minister to the nation only.

Because of "blindness" to the identity of God's people, Jacob-Israel most of our Christian ministers have taught erroneously that the Church's members form Christs' "Kingdom". This is only a half-true doctrine compared with the glorious reality The Book of Revelation states that those worthy to be chosen (the true Church of resurrected overcomers) by God to reign with Him DO NOT constitute the "Kingdom", but are "co-heirs" (the "Body of Christ") of the Kingdom, standing as "kings and Priests" who shall *live and reign with Him* (on the earth) *a thousand years"* (Compare Rev. 1:6; 5:10; 20:6).

On the other hand, the Kingdom over which Christ and His Body (the "Bridegroom") will reign is the earthly Messianic House of Jacob (the "Bride of Christ"), the latter destined to become a spiritual people ultimately. Of this Kingdom, God says: *"Behold, the days come, saith the Lord, when I will make a new covenant with the house of Israel and with the house of Judah: Not according to the covenant that I made with their fathers in the day when I took them out of the land of Egypt; because they continued not in my covenant and I regarded them not, saith the Lord. For this is the covenant that I will make with the house of Israel after those days, saith the Lord; I will put my laws into their mind, and write them in their hearts: and I will be to them a God, and they shall be to me a people:"* (Heb. 8:8-10).

Why is Christianity today, so blind to the truth of a coming Kingdom of God being made manifest on the earth? Why do they look to "heaven" as their future home? Is it because the church fails to recognize Christian American as God's "chosen people" Israel and His Stone Kingdom nation? If we dare to use the words "a chosen people", all boasting will be excluded if we remember that in the language of true religion, "chosen" means for service, perhaps even suffering, never for favouritism. Let us therefore thank God for the opportunity to serve Him in His great plan for humanity.

It should not be hard to see that God has kept His promises that He made to Jacob and his posterity. These promises of God have for the most part come to pass in Christian America. Dare we ignore His words that said: *"Ye are my witnesses, saith the Lord, and my servant whom I have chosen: that ye may know and believe me, and understand that I am he: before me there was no God formed, neither shall there be after me. I, even I, am the Lord; and beside me there is no saviour"* (Isa. 43: 10,11). *"This people have I formed for myself; they shall shew forth my praise"* (Isa. 43:21).

God is sending forth a call to the modern "House of Israel" (The United States of America—peopled by a gathering of all the thirteen tribes of Israel) to repent and learn of Him. By an example of obedience of His Laws they may prepare themselves to fulfill Christ's commission to lead the world to happiness, prosperity and a perpetual peace for all men and nations. *"The time is fulfilled, and the kingdom of God* (on earth) *is at hand: Repent ye, and believe the gospel"* (Mark 1:15).

In their "blindness" mankind has lost their way—they do not know the *"way of peace"* (Isa 59:8). Only when the glorious everlasting Kingdom of God, and His Government, is established on this earth, will man attain real peace—when the "Prince of Peace", in supernatural power and glory, sits upon Jacob's Pillar.

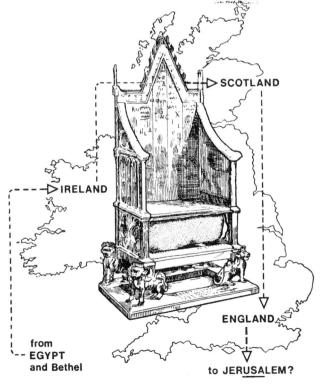

89

THE THRONE OF DAVID
TO BE
EVERLASTING

"Hail to the Lord's Anointed,
    Great David's greater son.
Hail in the time appointed,
    His reign on earth begun!
He comes to break oppression,
    To set the captive free,
To take away transgression,
    And rule in equity.

O'er every foe victorious,
    He on His throne shall rest;
From age to age more glorious,
    All-blessing and all-blest:
The time of tide shall never
    His covenant remove;
His Name shall stand for ever,
    His changeless Name of Love".

Following is a genealogical table from Abraham, showing the royal House of David. (Throne)

Abraham
Isaac
Jacob
Judah

Pharez	Zarah
Hezron (Ezron)	Ethan
Aram on Ram	Mahol
Amminadab	Calcol
Nahshon	Gadhol
Salma (Salmon)	Easru
Boaz	Sru
Obed	Heber Scot
Jesse	Boamhain
David (Throne established)	Ayhaimhain
Solomon	Tait
Rehoboam	Aghenoin
Abijah	Feabla Glas
Asa	Neanuail
Jehoshaphat	Nuaghadh
Jehoram	Alloid
Ahaziah	Earchada
Joash	Degffatha
Amaziah	Bratha
Azariah (Uzziah)	Broegan
Jotham	Bille
Ahaz	Gathelus (Gallam)
Hezekiah	
Manasseh	
Amon	
Josiah	
Zedekiah	
Scota (the Tender Twig)	

OVERTURNING

Eochaidh (Eremhon-Heremon) — Tamar Tephi (King & Queen of Ireland)
Irial Faidh
Eithriall
Prince Follain
Tighernmas
Prince Eanbotha
Prince Smiorguil
Fiachadh Labhruine (Labhriane)

Aongus Oilbhuagach
Prince Maoin
Rotheachta
Prince Dein
Iorna Saoghalach
Prince Oliolla Olchaoin
Giallchadh
Nuadha Fionn Fail
Simon Breac
Muriadhach Bolgrach
Fiachadh Tolgrach
Duach Laighrach
Prince Eochaidh Buillaig
Ugaine More (the Great)
Cobhthach Caolbreag
Prince Meilage
Jaran Gleofathach
Oiliolla Caisfhiaclach
Eochaid Foltleathan
Angus Tuirimheach (the Prolific)
Eanda Aighnach
Prince Labhra Luire
Prince Blathachta Eamhna
Prince Easamhuin Eamhna
Prince Roighneaim Ruadh
Prince Finlogha
Prince Finn
Eochaidh Fiedhlioch
Prince Bias Fineamhuas
Lughaidh Riebdearg (Raidhdearg)
Criomhthan (Crimthann) Niadhnar
Fioraidhach Fionfachtnach
Fiachadh Fionohudh
Tuathal Teachtman
Fiedhlimhidh Reachtmar
Conn Ceadchadhach
Art Aonfhir (the Melancholy)
Cormac Ulfhada
Cairbre Liffeachaire
Fiachadh Streabhthuine
Muirreadhach Tireach
Eochaidh Moihmeodhain
Niall (of the Nine Hostages)
Prince Eogan
Prince Muireadhach
Mortough

OVERTURNING

Fergus More - King of Argyll (Scotland)
Fiachra
Fergus I
Manius
Dornadil
Reuthar
Edars (Edersced)
(Birth of Christ)
Conaire the Great
Corbred I
Corbred II
Modha Lamha
Corbred Dalriada
Eochaidh
Findachar
Thrinklind
Fincornack
Romaich
Angus
Eochaidh
Erc
Fergus the Great
Dongard
Conran (Guvran)
Aidan (Aydan)
Eugene IV
Donald IV
Prince Dobgard (Donregarth)
Eugene IV
Prince Findan
Eugene V
Ethafind
Achaias (Ethas)
Alpin
Kenneth I - King of Scotland
Constantin
Donald II
Malcolm I
Kenneth II
Malcolm II
Princess Beatrix
Duncan I
Malcolm III (Caenmore)
David I
Prince Henry
David, Earl of Huntingdon
Isobel Huntingdon
Lord Robert Bruce

Robert the Bruce I
Princess Marjory Bruce
Robert II
Robert III
James I
James II
James III
James IV
James V
Mary, Queen of Scots - Queen of Scotland

OVERTURNING

James VI and I - King of Great Britain
Princess Elizabeth Stewart
Princess Sophia
George I
George II
Prince Frederick of Wales
George III
Edward, Duke of Kent
Queen Victoria
Edward VII
George V
George VI
Elizabeth II

ISRAEL'S POEM

Now may God of power and grace
Attend His people's humble cry;
Jehovah hears when Israel prays,
And brings deliverance from on high.
The name of Jacob's God defends,
Better than shields and brazen walls;
He, from His sanctuary sends
Succour and strength when Zion calls.
Well, He remembers all our sighs;
His love exceeds our best deserts;
His love accepts the sacrifice
Of humble groans and broken hearts.

In His salvation is our hope.
And in the Name of Israel's God;
Our troops shall lift their banners up,
Our navies spread their flags abroad.
Some trust in horses trained for war,
And some of chariots make their boast;
Our surest expectations are
From thee, the Lord of heavenly hosts.
Now save us, Lord, from slavish fear;
Now let our hopes be firm and strong;
Till thy salvation shall appear,
And joy and triumph raise the song.

Isaac Watts (1674-1748)

The
Coronation
Chair
and
Screen

Herbert Railton

The
Stone
Scone

Artisan books are unique! Thanks to Artisan Publishers many rare and unusual books are now back in print. Several of these books are by scholars who, through much study and research, discovered some astonishing truths when they combined Biblical history and prophecy with archaeology and secular history!

DIGITAL EDITION

PUBLISHED BY

ARTISAN PUBLISHERS
P.O. Box 1529
Muskogee, Oklahoma 74402
(918) 682-8341
www.artisanpublishers.com

PUBLISHER

ARTISAN PUBLISHERS
A Subsidiary of HOFFMAN PRINTING CO.
P.O. Box 1529 · Muskogee, Oklahoma 74402
Phone (918) 682-8341 · www.artisanpublishers.com

BOOKS BY E. RAYMOND CAPT

"Abrahamic Covenant"
"Petra"
"Jacob's Pillar"
"Our Great Seal" Expanded Edition
"Study of Pyramidology"
"The Glory of the Stars"
"King Solomon's Temple"
"Great Pyramid Decoded"
"Olivet Prophecies"
"Isle of Iona"
"Counterfeit Christianity"

"Stonehenge and Druidism"
"The Traditions of Glastonbury"
"The Gem Stones In The Breastplate"
"Lost Chapter of Acts of the Apostles"
"The Scottish Declaration of Independence"
"Missing Links Discovered In Assyrian Tablets"
"The Resurrection Tomb"
"Biblical Antiquities" I, II, III, IV, V, VI
"The Stone Kingdom, America"
"Paul the Missionary"

AUDIO - CASSETTES / CDs by E. Raymond Capt

"Biblical Antiquities" I, II, III, IV

VIDEO - VHS TAPES / DVDs by E. Raymond Capt

"The Coming of the Saints"
"Faith of Our Fathers"
"The Glory of the Stars"
"The Great Pyramid Decoded"
"King Solomon's Temple"
"Petra, and As Birds Flying"
"Planting the Faith Westward"
"Sinai, A Closer Look"

"Stone of Destiny"
"Strange Parallel"
"They Came A-Viking"
"Traditions of Glastonbury"
"America's Godly Heritage"
"The California Missions Story"
"The Creation of a Nation"
"Megalith Builders"

OTHER PUBLICATIONS

"America B.C."
"Christianity and the Age of the Earth"
"The Origin of Christianity in Britain"
"The Message of the Minor Prophets"
"Stories of Lost Israel in Folklore"
"The Post Captivity Names of Israel"
"Revelation of St. John the Divine"
"On the Track of the Exodus"
"Israel Kingdom Scriptures"
"Dan the Pioneer of Israel"
"The Abrahamic Covenant"
"Statesmanship of Jesus"
"Our Heritage: The Bible"
"Coming of the Saints"
"The Soul of Cambria"
"Dedicated Disciples"
"Prehistoric London"
"As Birds Flying"
"The Assyrian Invasions and Deportations of Israel"
"Differences - Bible vs The Koran"
"Lost Tribes of Israel"
"The Rapture Plot"

"St. Paul in Britain"
"Strange Parallel"
"The Names of God"
"Book of Jubilees"
"Book of Enoch"
"Book of Jasher"
"Saint George"
"Isaiah - A Study"
"Bible Stories for Children"
"Celt, Druid and Culdee"
"Far Above Rubies"
"Iceland's Great Inheritance"
"Jesus Christ Triumphant"
"The Rapture of the Saints"
"The Restitution of All Things"
"Tracing Our Ancestors"
"The USA in Bible Prophecy"
"The Stones Cry Out"
"Jesus of Nazareth"
"Thy Kingdom Come"
"Noah's Ark - The Evidence"
"The Lost Books of the Bible & the Forgotten Books of Eden"